VISUAL MERCHANDISING

FROM THE EDITORS OF *VM+SD* MAGAZINE

ST PUBLICATIONS
CINCINNATI, OHIO

ISBN: 0-944094-24-4

Published by:
ST Publications, Inc.
Book Division
407 Gilbert Avenue
Cincinnati, Ohio 45202
Tel. 513-421-2050
Fax 513-421-6110

Distributed to the book and art trade
in the U.S. and Canada by:
Watson-Guptill Publications
1515 Broadway
New York, NY 10036
Tel. 908-363-4511
Fax 908-363-0338

Distributed to the rest of the world by:
Hearst Books International
1350 Avenue of the Americas
New York, NY 10003
Tel. 212-261-6770
Fax 212-261-6795

Book design by Carole Winters

Printed in Hong Kong

10 9 8 7 6 5 4 3 2 1

TABLE OF CONTENTS

HOME FURNISHINGS

Nowhere outside of the home furnishing department is it possible to group so many different types of merchandise together in lifestyle presentations. Furniture at Pottery Barn or Amapola can be presented together in coordinating vignettes with rugs, decoratives, china, silver, light fixtures, plants and draperies. Williams-Sonoma can gather large ceramic bowls together on a table with pasta, sauces, vinegars, cooking implements and cloth napkins. Noritake can place an entire china collection on damask cloths with silver, china and plate stands, ornamented with greenery and loaves of bread. ◆ All create a careful fusion of fantasy and reality in demonstrating how furnishings could look in customers' own homes. Some of the most effective window presentation, however, go a step farther to combine elements from the home that traditionally aren't seen together. CMI's presentation of silver patterns atop plant stands, for example, or Pfaltzgraff's use of flatware as an architectural cornice above hat-box "towers." ◆ You'll notice considerable attention paid to materials and surface treatments in this chapter — faux-finished walls; sponged and brushed tiles for flooring and backdrops; fabrics draped luxuriously as space dividers or backdrops; fine steel mesh coiled to provide a setting for fine china and silver. ◆ Dramatic lighting provides the final detail for these residential vignettes. You'll see lighting plans designed to highlight the handrubbed glow of wood furniture finishes, the transparency of glass and the shining brilliance of silver. Residential-style pendant and tables lamps serve as accents.

Pottery Barn, San Francisco

5

POTTERY BARN CHESTNUT STREET
SAN FRANCISCO

Foster Cope III, director; Richard Altuna, Los Angeles, designer; Parry Yohannen, visual merchandising director; Howard Backen, BAR (Backen, Arrigoni & Ross), principal in charge; Hans Baldauf, BAR, project manager; Williams-Sonoma Store Development team: Gary Friedman, president; Patti Kashima, design manager; Danielle Curelli, project manager; Scott Johnson, construction coordinator; Ellen De Forest, assistant to the director

◆

The theme of this store is timelessness. The simplicity of materials and blend of custom and natural lighting make it possible. Unfinished birdhouses function as the imaginary canvas between color cards and the paint products below (photo on this page). Directly behind the cashwrap is the Design Studio (photo on opposite page) with its custom pendandt light fixtures. In the back of the store a set of windows allows for sunlight to shine on sofas, creating an ideal effect for the customer.

◆

Audio/Visual: Pacific Rim, Sausalito, Calif.; Fixturing: Environments, Inc., Minnetonka, Minn.; Flooring: Golden State Flooring; Lighting: Neidhardt, Inc., San Francisco, and American Wholesale Lighting, Fremont, Calif.; Signage: Thomas Swan Signs, San Francisco; Joe Farais, Oakland, custom metalwork; Buddy Rhodes, San Francisco, fabricators

DOUG DUN, BAR, SAN FRANCISCO

AMAPOLA
NORTH POINT CENTER
FRESNO, CALIF.

Bob Benson, visual merchandising director; Anthony De Leon and Brian Redfern, store team

◆

To draw attention to the change in merchandise from contemporary giftware to custom upholstery and furniture, the whole store was draped in dropcloths of mismatched white damask remnants and seconds with cotton bullion upholstery fringe. A graphic border with famous quotes on style and design was added to the ceiling/grid line. These photos are from early March, just before the store's "Founder's Day Sale."

◆

Painted floor: Karl Jensen, Fresno, Calif.; Plants: Living Green, Fresno, Calif.; Silk flowers: Wynward Silks; Regal International Fabrics: Aubusson Textile, New York City; Bart Halpern, New York City

TAMELA RYATT, RYATT PHOTOGRAPHY, KINGSBURY, CALIF.

ALICE
THE CARPET STUDIO
DENVER DESIGN CENTER
DENVER

Jacquelyn Noble and Steven Erickson,
Noble-Erickson, Inc., Denver,
visual merchandising directors

◆

This display recreates a famous
scene from Alice in Wonderland.
The angle of the table and chair,
with their tea set defying gravity,
imparts movement, while the
scene is partially reflected by the
fabric-draped mirror.

◆

Fabric: Jack Lenor Larsen, New York
City

STEVEN ERICKSON, DENVER

WILLIAMS-SONOMA SOHO
NEW YORK CITY

Foster Cope III, director of store development, Williams-Sonoma Inc., San Francisco; Richard Altuna, Los Angeles, designer; Cynde Lanna, visual merchandising director; Howard Backen, BAR (Backen, Arrigoni & Ross, San Francisco), principal in charge; Hans Baldauf, BAR, project manager

◆

Custom-pendant light fixtures and track lighting bring out the lightness of the natural wood finish. Tables interspersed among ceiling columns offer bread, baskets and wine. Glassware and flatware face out from the shelves against the walls.

◆

Fixturing: Environments, Inc., Minnetonka, Minn.; Lighting: Neidhardt, Inc., San Francisco, and American Wholesale Lighting, Fremont, Calif.; Signage: Thomas Swan Signs, San Francisco; Joe Farais, Oakland and Buddy Rhodes, San Francisco, fabricators

FALL TABLETOP SHOWS
NORITAKE CO., INC. SHOWROOM, NEW YORK CITY

Edward A. Lent, designer and visual merchandising director

◆

Each display of Noritake's tabletop patterns is designed to provide buyers ideas on how to accessorize the pieces in their own stores. Color and texture are enhanced by dramatic props, interior elements, furnishings and textiles that reflect lifestyle and suggest placement.

◆

Suppliers: ABC Carpet and Home, New York City; George Dell, New York City; Elevations, San Francisco; Home Depot, Fairfield, Conn.; Vogue International, Los Angeles

BRIDAL PARTY
Saturday, February 10, 1 to 5 p.m., Salt Lake Downtown store only

DENNIS POTTS, SALT LAKE CITY

BRIDAL PARTY
ZCMI
SALT LAKE CITY

Mike Stephens, visual director;
Diane Call, designer;
Gary Myers, project team.

Silver patterns were featured as part of a store-wide bridal promotion. Sponged and brushed wooden tiles were used on the floor and wall. Plant stands, painted a solid green, support white hands that hold nine different silver patterns.

◆

Lighting: Halo Lighting, Elk Grove Village, Ill.

PFALTZGRAFF

DAVID WHITE, NEW YORK CITY

SILVER SPRING
PFALTZGRAFF SHOWROOM
NEW YORK CITY

Stephen Wagner, visual merchandising director; Stefano Corradi, Deborah Paley,
Susan Smith and David White, project team

Vertical urban elements combine with country details to introduce floral
dinnerware collections. The towers are chicken wire mesh wrapped
around hat boxes. Each in a series of six windows features a different
color hat box, coordinating with the dinnerware. Nuts and bolts support
the hat box lids, creating different levels of merchandise. Flatware is
used as an architectural cornice atop the towers, two towers in each
window are topped by an imaginary garden of daisies. At eye level in
each window, two towers topped with five-piece place settings and
compatible glassware suggest a picnic. A picket fence, built of wood
frame and fine mesh screen, serves as a backdrop in each window.
Silver butterflies cling to the screen, creating a feeling of light, air and
movement.

◆

Folding screen: Julin & Larrabee Design, New York City; Hat boxes: Viaggio Inc.,
W. Babylon, N.Y.

IKEA'S MARKETING OUTPOST
NEW YORK CITY

WalkerGroup/CNI, New York City:
Patricia Oris, principal in charge;
Renata Zednicek, project manager;
Diego Garay, Derick Hudspith,
Steven Kitezh, Michael Ross and
David Wales, project design team

◆

The objective of the "outpost" is
to define the store as a total
resource for all home furnishing
needs. To accomplish this, the
designer created a "stage set"
that could be changed every six
weeks to feature a different
major product classification, such
as cookware or sleep
accessories. Everything is
changeable, including the walls,
cabinets, cashwraps and all
graphics. An eight-foot grid
system of moving walls was
developed, consisting of a
structural metal ceiling grid from
which wooden panels are hung.
The grid also incorporates
movable track lighting. Tapping
into the store's simple image,
materials include blond woods,
concrete flooring and natural
finishes. Graphic panels are
blue, yellow and white (the
store's colors) with simple type.

◆

General contractor: The Stegla
Group, Inc., New York City;
Fixturing: Alpha Display Co., Inc.,
Bronx, N.Y. (grid merchandise
display system); S&G Woodwork,
Brooklyn, N.Y. (juice bar, cashwrap
and loose fixtures); Audio: AEI Music,
Seattle; Plastic shelving inserts:
Industrial Plastics, New York City;
Mezzanine glass: Bendheim Glass,
New York City

DOROTHÉE AHRENS, NEW YORK CITY

LIFESTYLE

Whether our leisure time is spent at home, eating out or at special events, we expect to be entertained. Among the businesses that cater to these demands are retailers of entertainment products, on-location gift stores, restaurants and themed environments. Retailers including Blockbuster, B. Dalton Kids and Borders Books & Music provide customers with books, tapes and videos to take home. ◆ CBS' retail store and the Official All-Star Cafe entice visitors to purchase memorabilia of their visits. Other retailers, like Spencer Gifts' new Glow! concept and Candymania candy stores, make it their business to make the act of shopping for candy — or glow-in-the-dark toys and accessories — an entertaining process. And Tempus Expeditions is one in the new and growing category of mall-based combined entertainment and educational themed

environments, with a retail sales area located conveniently near the cinematic ride's exit. ◆ These interiors don't stint on the special effects — light, sound and interactivity. You'll find a wide variety of theatrical lighting effects, neon, moving sculptures, sound effects and video. Tempus Expeditions recreates the workshop of a mad scientist, complete with clockwork gears, glowing yellow neon and various other mechanical "inventions." Glow! lights its space primarily with black-light projectors, making the interior of the store glow with the unearthly UV-reactive colors of its merchandise. Candymania creates a "candy-land" fantasy land for children with colorful and unusual-shaped fixtures, a curving "road" that leads through the space and full-height candy display tubes against the walls, all geared toward making the experience special — and making the sale.

Tempus Expeditions, Mall of America

19

And one man in his time
They have their exits and their entrances;
the whining schoolboy with
plays many parts.
Then
shining morning
a woeful ballad Made to his mistress'
quarrel, Seeking the
And then the justice, Full of wise
the lean and slippered
childish treble. Last scene
and mere
and future can be

DAN FORER, MIAMI

TEMPUS EXPEDITIONS
MALL OF AMERICA
BLOOMINGTON, MINN.

FRCH Design Worldwide, Cincinnati: James Fitzgerald, chair and ceo; Kevin Roche, partner-in-charge; Mike Beeghly, principal-in-charge; Steve McGowan, senior project designer; Tom Horwitz, project director; Romano Klepec, Les Bradford, Chip Williamson, production assistants; Laira Bogner, design assistant; Laura Lee, graphic designer.
Tempus Expeditions team: William Sadleir, president; Rosalind Nowicki, co-director of merchandise; Kimcee McAnally, director of organizational development

◆

Combining entertainment, education and retailing, this mall store's main attraction is a motion simulator ride that chronicles human ingenuity. The logo appears on storefront, labeling, packaging, stationery, shopping bags and a wide assortment of branded goods. Collaterals were carefully developed to complement the interior design. The 2,300-square-foot retail area is designed to capture customers before and after they experience the motion simulator ride.

◆

General contractor: Fortney & Wegandt, Lakewood, Ohio; Fixturing: JPM, Eden Prairie, Minn.; Siewert, Minneapolis; Flooring: Bentley, Oklahoma City (carpet); Mannington Commercial, Calhoun, Ga. (tile); Toli Int'l., Commack, N.Y. (tile); Forbo, Hazelton, Pa.; Viking Terrazo Company, Minneapolis, (terrazo); Lighting: Lighting Management Inc., New City, N.Y.; Special Finish: Marlite, Dover, Ohio; Wall coverings: Archetonic, Yonkers, N.Y.; Blumenthal, Long Island City, N.Y.; Anya Larkin, New York City; Innovations, New York City; Fabrics: Unika Vaev, Orangeburg, N.Y.; HBF Textiles, Long Island City, N.Y.; HGH Design Group, San Francisco; Signage/graphics: Kieffer & Co., Marietta, Ga. (storefront); 3M, Minneapolis (graphics on storefront); Sterling, Cincinnati (fixture logo fabricator); Mannequins/props: Greneker, Los Angeles; Special equipment: Moog Inc., East Aurora, N.Y. (simulator); Triad Systems, Des Moines, Iowa (show control); Sony Electronics, Montvale, N.J. (high definition visual); High Performance Stereo, Boston (surround sound); Dream Quest Images, Simi Valley, Calif. (film production); Blumberg Communications, Minneapolis (projection screens); M-E Engineering, Columbus, Ohio (engineers).

CANDYMANIA
LAS VEGAS HILTON HOTEL
LAS VEGAS

Schafer Associates Design team, Oakbrook Terrace, Ill.: Barry Vinyard, president and creative director; Beth Howley, project director; David Koe, project designer. Candymania, Las Vegas: Steve Shaiken, regional vice president, retail.

◆

Created as a signature licensed brand for Hilton Hotels Corporation, Candymania's 730-square-foot space took a graphic approach with bright colors and shapes. Rounded edges and sloping fixtures highlight the confectionery merchandise. Clear acrylic tubes — spanning from the ceiling halfway down the wall — are filled with artificial product designed to look as if the bins below are gravity fed. The use of primary colors on surfaces and flooring complements the rainbow of colors found in the store's product.

◆

Project architect: Design Core, Inc., Las Vegas; General contractor: Harris Associates, Las Vegas; Fixtures: Woodmasters, Addison, Ill.; Tile: Amtico, Atlanta; Paint: Sherwin Williams, Cleveland, and Benjamin Moore, Montvale, N.J.; Laminates: Abet Laminati, Englewood, N.J.; Lighting: Abolite Neuveaux, Cincinnati

THE CBS STORE
NEW YORK CITY

Design: Rockwell Group, New York City. David Rockwell, principal; Jeff Harris, project manager; Ian Circhall, operations director; Randy Morton, designer; Alice Yiu, director of interiors; Eve-lynn Schoenstein, interior designer.
CBS, Inc., Marc D. Chiapperino, P.E.

◆

Images of icons from the Golden Age of television — Jackie Gleason and Lucille Ball, to name two — share space with current personalities at the CBS Store in New York City's Ed Sullivan Theater. In fact the 300-square-foot store's color scheme, red and green, are based on Lucy's hair and Ethel's green dress. The primary communicators in and out of the store are, not surprisingly, vintage to contemporary television sets. Outside the store, television sets are embedded in the sidewalk to entertain those waiting in line.

◆

Cabinetry and millwork: Yan's Fine Woodworking, Maspeth, N.Y. Lighting design: Focus Lighting, New York City, Paul Gregory and Diana Schlenk, designers. Lighting: Tivoli, Santa Ana, Calif. (track lighting); Lucifer Lighting, San Antonio, Texas, (edge-lit shelf lighting); DSA Phototech, Los Angeles (light boxes); Itre, Brooklyn, N.Y. (marquee colored star downlights). Signage: County Neon, New York City. Materials: Nevamar, Odenton, Md. (laminate); Formica, Cincinnati (laminate); All City Glass, Brooklyn, N.Y. (glass and stainless steel). Sound and motor installation: Robert Brock, Westchester, N.Y.; CMS AV Consultant, Long Island, N.Y. Storefront: Ellison Door, Falconer, N.Y.

PAUL WARCHOL, NEW YORK CITY

BORDERS BOOKS AND MUSIC
UNION SQUARE
SAN FRANCISCO

FRCH Design Worldwide, Cincinnati

◆

Where Borders' signage and graphics previously varied from store to store, the new comprehensive program provides a consistent image for the first time. The new logo can stand alone or with the exuberant dancing figures created to express the company's love of books and music. The logo is applied to everything from banners on the building facade to bookmarks, shopping bags, stickers, packaging, catalogs and gift certificates. Custom giftwrap and a selection of branded merchandise (coffee mugs and T-shirts) rounds out the graphics package.

◆

Graphics: Advent Designs, Groveport, Ohio; Sullivan & Brampton, San Leandro, Calif.; Transport Graphics, San Francisco

PAMELA MONFORT PHOTOGRAPHY, CINCINNATI

MICHAEL ROSEN, BAINBRIDGE ISLAND, WASH.

B. DALTON KIDS
WASHINGTON SQUARE
TIGARD, ORE.

Design: NBBJ Retail Concepts, Seattle. Keith L. Smith, project manager; James O. Jonassen, ceo; Lisa T. Hudson, visual merchandising director; James Adams, principal in charge; James Adams, Chris St. Aubyn, Liz Gramryd, Stacy Weisbroth, Michael Thomas, Samantha Dorfman and David Nickelson, project team.

◆

The challenge was to seamlessly meld the children's and adult sections of the store without making the transition obvious. Books, matching colors, materials, finishes and the masses of the two storefronts all play a key role in the seamless separation. Characters coming out of books at the storefront create an illusion and fantasy for both younger children and adults. Using recognizable characters aided in subtly defining the two spaces.

◆

Audio/visual: AEI, Inc., Seattle; Fixturing: Excell, Toronto; Flooring: Associated Flooring, New York City; Lighting: Lighting Management, New York City; Signage: Midtown Neon, New York City; Graphics: Engraphix, St. Louis; Props: Design Fabricators, Lafayette, Colo.; Storefront: Ontario Store Fixtures, Weston, Ont.

BLOCKBUSTER
FT. LAUDERDALE, FLA.

Fitch, Inc., Boston: Paul Lechleiter and Mark Artus, project managers; Matthew Napoleon, client liaison; Maribeth Gatchalian, Paul Harlor, Scott Richardson, Beth Dorsey, Kelly Moony, Alycia Freeman, Fred Weaver, Ed Chung and Jeff Pacione, graphics; Sarah DeLeon, implementation.
Blockbuster, Ft. Lauderdale, Fla.: Karen Yokel, director of store planning; Corry Oakes, director of construction; John Tombari, AIA, special projects manager; Jim Hilmer, director of marketing (formerly of Blockbuster)

◆

Key focal points in this space are identified by large visual graphics appealing to the emotional aspects of Hollywood, filmmaking and a night at the movies. Dynamic forms and a high-technology presence combine with a simplified signage system to construct a layering of messages to consumers. Different signed areas around the store's interior — "Lights, Camera, Action," "You ain't seen nothing yet" and "What's Hot" — all combine with new flooring, fixturing and ceiling treatments creating a dramatic new look for the store.

◆

Lighting: Lighting Management, Inc., New York City. Signs (exterior and center area): Art Sign Company, Ft. Lauderdale, Fla. Sign letters (interior): Chandler Signs, Dallas. Graphics (photo): Aperture, Boston. Ceiling baffles: Wyko-Mica Products, Ft. Lauderdale, Fla.

MARK STEELE, FITCH INC., BOSTON

GLOW!
CITYWALK
UNIVERSAL CITY, CALIF.

Design: Richard Altuna, Los Angeles; Spencer Gifts Inc., Egg Harbor Township, N.J. — John Hacala, president and ceo; Ken Garagiola, divisional vice president, real estate; Daniel Richeal, visual merchandising manager; Doug Orloff, general manager; Bob Henderson, divisional vice president, construction; Clay Chaffin, director of marketing; Tim Clare, Joe Deluca, Shelby Bell and Bob Richardson, design team

◆

The dark and intriguing atmosphere of Spencer Gifts' new concept utilizes inexpensive materials such as pine, sheetrock and cement that are either accented with UV-reactive paint or obscured altogether with flat black paint. A combination of UV light and incandescent sources balance ambient lighting needs against the backlight special effects. Products in the 1,100-square-foot area include glow-in-the-dark clothes, stationery, jewelry, art, toys and gifts.

◆

Visual consultant: Cynthia Mendel, Oakland, Calif.; Lighting, special effects and signage: Michael Friedman and Richard Green, Wildfire, Los Angeles; Graphic design: Chad White, Sauce Design, Los Angeles; Fixturing and furniture: CDL Cabinet & Fixture, Pacoima, Calif.; Mannequins and forms: Acme Display Fixture Co., Los Angeles

BUD COSBY, SPENCER GIFTS INC., EGG HARBOR TOWNSHIP, N.J.; AND WILDFIRE INC., LOS ANGELES

OFFICIAL ALL-STAR CAFE
NEW YORK CITY

◆

Rockwell Architecture, Planning and Design, New York City: David Rockwell, principal; Ian Birchall and Chris Smith, associates-in-charge; Anne Corvi, project manager; David Mexico and Jay Valgora, design team; Claire Baldwin, Lorraine Knapp and Lisa Pope, interiors; Mimi Kuch, Oswaldo Brighenti, Jeff Harris, Dan Kocieniewski, Tim Nanni and Martin Weiner, staff

◆

"Being There" is the theme in this rich, fun-filled sport environment. The experience is enhanced by glove-leather seats, sports memorabilia and video screens viewable from virtually any angle. The 40,000-square-foot space also incorporates live sports feeds from the television networks, cable channels, international satellites and real-time celebrity interviews. Interactive television and virtual-reality video heighten customers' sense of "Being There." The merchandise presentation area continues in the sports theme with muted tones and natural wood finishes. Also, so those waiting for merchandise won't miss a minute of sports action, video screens have been positioned behind the counters.

Millwork: Superior Architectural, Forest Hills, N.Y.; Displays: Orlando Corporate Services, Orlando, Fla. (memorabilia displays); ASI, Jersey City, N.J. (diorama); Unique Wood Designs, Altamonte Springs, Fla. (display cases); Signage: Custom Sign, Eldon, Mo. (interior and exterior signs); Seating: Artcraft, Orlando, Fla.; Flooring: USAX, Greenville, Miss. (custom carpet); DESSO Carpets, Paoli, Pa. (custom carpet); Hartco Wood Flooring, Knoxville, Texas; No Fault Industries, Baton Rouge, La. (resilient); Paint: Benjamin Moore, Montvale, N.J.; Pratt & Lambert, Buffalo, N.Y.; Specialty painting: Modeworks, New York City; Sound/video: Soundelux, Orlando, Fla.

◆

VENDOR CONCEPTS

"Communicating the brand" continues to grow in importance. Increased competition for consumer dollars means that brands are investing in differentiating themselves in shop concepts, outlet stores or highly visible manufacturer showplaces. Successful vendors — Levi's, Haggar or OshKosh B'Gosh apparel; Microsoft computer software; Sony electronics; Reebok shoes; and even BMW Roadsters — take a comprehensive look at their brand identity and use every means at their disposal to communicate image to their customers. ◆ Consider Sony's coordinated and comprehensive approach, beginning with its showplace Sony Style store concept in Manhattan. This, together with coordinated advertising and frequently changing window displays, promotes product sales through Sony's own store and through more traditional distributors. Graphics play a vital role in vendor concepts, from lifestyle photography in

Levi stores to point-of-purchase video in Microsoft's interactive stations. BMW Roadsters are placed against huge backdrop murals of roadside scenery, with blue skies overhead. In Haggar's outlet store, posters and video promote the casual attitude of the company's "Stuff You Can Wear" campaign. ◆ Visual elements and props — bowling balls, tin cans, license plates, old suitcases and billiard balls — continue the "everyday" theme. You'll notice that vendor branding messages infuse every aspect of the interiors in this chapter. Guess' "authentic American style" manifests itself through American Arts and Crafts architectural detailing, woods finished with hand-rubbed linseed oil finishes, Shaker crates and a massive, reassuring maple cashwrap. Levi, on the other hand, supports its "personal pair" custom fit program through comfortable seating in the sales area and computers in the dressing rooms.

The Disney Store, New York City

THE DISNEY STORE
NEW YORK CITY

The Disney Store, Inc., Walt Disney Imagineering,
and Elkus/Manfredi Architects, Boston

◆

Disney's New York City flagship store is meant to resemble a
"home away from home" for Disney characters. Dreamlike colors
enhance the feel of a cartoonish interior landscape. Closetlike alcoves
house children's apparel. Fixturing and architecture in the flagship store
of the Disney store evoke the studio's classic animated features.
A video wall designed to recall the porthole from the Nautilus in
"20,000 Leagues under the Sea" has a dramatic presence on the
second floor. The cast-fiberglass video surround was created by
Disney craftsmen and faux finished.

"MAGIC LINK"
SONY PLAZA
NEW YORK CITY

Sony, New York City — Christine Belich, creative director; LeighAnn Tischler, visual merchandising; Tammy Stubbs, graphics. Maira Kalman, New York City.

◆

Here, three "wireheaded mannequins" convey the message of an "electronified" existence. "Isidor" wears a jacket of compact discs (from Sony artists, of course) to express his love of music. Finally, a Kalman mannequin by Pucci sports a period costume to promote the video release of the period drama "Sense and Sensibility." On the following pages, one window employs a Kalman-designed Pucci mannequin clad in phone message slips, overwhelmed by life, to promote Magic Link's memory. Another uses a mannequin with an "abrasive" personality (and scouring pad jacket to match) to catch the eye.

◆

Mannequins: Pucci Int'l., New York City. Props: Mark Turnage, New York City. Mannequin clothing: Rod Keenan, New York City (hats); Jim Sauli, New York City (paper clothing); Amy Franks, Pleasantville, N.Y. (other clothing). Murals: Jeanine Gerding, New York City

FRAN SOLOMAN, NEW YORK CITY

"MAGIC LINK"
SONY PLAZA
NEW YORK CITY

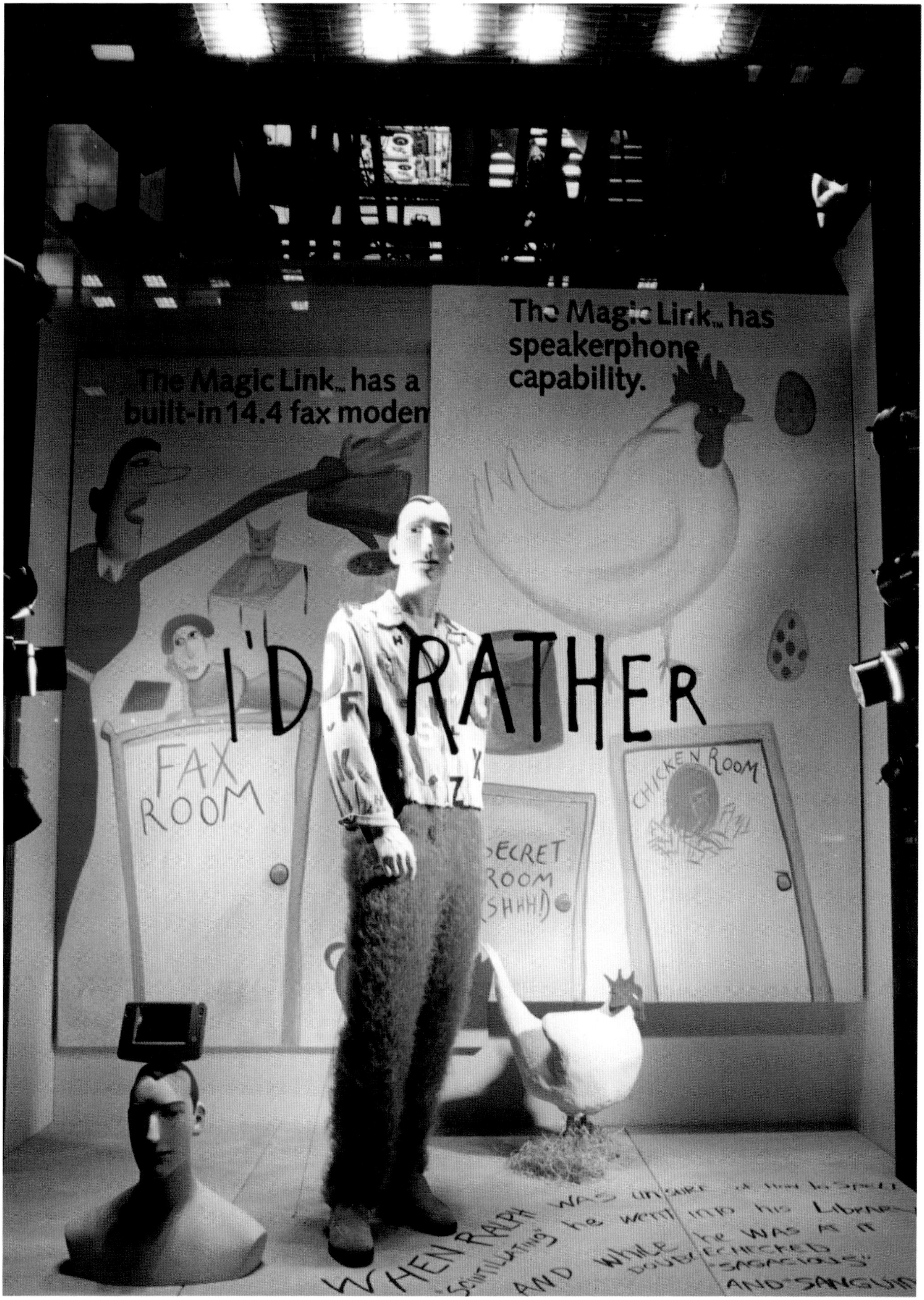

FRAN SOLOMAN, NEW YORK CITY

HAGGAR OUTLET STORE
BIRCH RUN, MICH.

FRCH Design Worldwide, Cincinnati

◆

In conjunction with a major repositioning and broadening of its product line, this menswear apparel manufacturer opened its first outlet stores last spring. Industrial-looking fixtures feature exposed studs and wooden closet doors as endcaps; clothing is hung on metal hooks instead of presented on mannequins; and fitting rooms of corrugated fiberglass boast bare light bulbs. The 4,000-square-foot seating area in the center of the store includes chairs with exposed backs, a table with garden-hose feet and a couch made from the trunk of a 1957 Chevy.

◆

Fixtures: MET Merchandising Concepts, Chicago; Hamilton Fixtures, Cincinnati (sign holders) Signage: PLI, Cincinnati (restroom/fitting room signs); Adex, Cincinnati (cloth banners) Decoratives: Precision Digital, Cincinnati (framed photos); Photographic Specialties, New York City (large-scale photos)

BMW SHOWROOM
SPARTANBURG, N.C.

Retail Planning Associates, L.P., Columbus, Ohio: Doug Cheesman, president; Jane Zulandt, director visual merchandising and design studies; Michele Kreber, vice president creative; Diane Rambo, vice president retail branding; John Rendleman, vice president implementation; Paul Hamilton, designer; Steve Sukolics, implementation manager

◆

Highlighting the introduction of the new BMW Roadster, this project presentation was created to allow customers to gather information without assistance from a sales associate. Providing access to information on a 24-hour basis, customers can even conduct financing activities through two-way interactive video. Large-scale graphic scrims include imagery that distinguishes the characteristics between various lines of BMW products. Accessories, recently introduced to the dealership environment, were placed in adjacencies for maximum exposure.

◆

Suppliers: Retail Planning Associates, Columbus, Ohio

MICROSOFT
NEBRASKA FURNITURE MART
OMAHA, NEBRASKA

Retail Planning Associates, L.P., Columbus, Ohio: Mike Bills, vice president; Linda Rosine, vice president; Vince Notaroberto, senior merchandiser/planner; Perry Kotnick, lighting manager; Edd Johns, senior consultant; Conrad Chin, designer; Tim Smith, vice president, communications; Adam Limbach, graphic designer; Diane Rambo, vice president, retail branding.
Microsoft: Carol Jen Drezak, Amy Anderson, Rebecca Kotch and Ed Belleba

◆

Designed to encourage curiosity and interactivity, this new shop simplifies software shopping by offering access to Microsoft's full product line and its features. Ceiling-suspended curved graphic panels define department boundaries, while mobilized light wood and stainless steel fixtures allow easy configuration and product mixing. Interactive kiosks are integrated into the merchandising system.

◆

Flooring: PermaGrain Products, Inc., Media, Pa. (wood); Laminates: Formica Corp., Cincinnati (plastic); The October Co., Inc., Easthampton, Mass. (plastic); Wilsonart, Temple, Texas (metal); Special Finishes: Herberts Powder Coatings, Hilliard, Ohio; Matrix Fixtures, Inc., Hastings on Hudson, N.Y.; Tiger Drylac U.S.A. Inc, Woodinville, Wash.

JERRY WISLER/APCOM, DAYTON, OHIO

PLANET REEBOK
NEW YORK CITY

Fitch, Inc., Worthington, Ohio: Beth Dorsey, project manager; Matthew Napoleon, Kelly Mooney, Christian Davies, Carol Dean, Kian Huat Kuan, Clint Bova, Doug Smith and Randy Miller.
Reebok International: Saul Gold, vice president, creative services; Larry Gore, vice president and general manager, retail division; Andrea Cassano, program manager.
C.I.T.E. Design, New York City (collaborated in development of graphic elements and implementation of design)

◆

The 4,500-square-foot retail space features an interactive window display and interactive kiosk in the center of the space. Footwear is prominently located along the main aisle, segmented by gender and sport. The curvy main aisle is lined by custom fixtures holding the newest shoes accompanied by informative video and graphics. Fixtures are light woods accented by powdercoated metals.

◆

Architect: Barry Koretz & Associates, Brockton, Mass.; General Contractors: GC Contractors, New York City; Fixture Manufacturer: PAM International, Saddle Brook, N.J.; Lighting: Windsor, Brooklyn, N.Y. (custom lighting elements); Lightolier, Seacaucus, N.J. (standard lighting elements); Lighting Management), New City, N.Y. (lighting elements; Lighting consultant: Euchromia Lighting, Kettering, Ohio; Flooring: Amtico, Atlanta; Interactive window display: Planet Interactive, Boston

THERE IS AN ATHLETE IN ALL OF US.

eXtra

STARTER VENDOR CONCEPT SHOP
DICK'S SPORTING GOODS
MONROEVILLE, PA.

Mobius, Inc., Eugene, Ore.: Peter Craycroft, principal in charge; Brad
Berman, project director; Craig Wollen, design director; Gary Hale, fixture
designer and engineer; Jennifer Fowell, merchandising
Graphic Design: Sally Morrow, Sandstrom Design, Portland, Ore.

◆

The Starter Corporation, makers of team licensed and branded
sports apparel, targeted men ages 12 to 34 in its first concept shop.
In a dark, neutral environment, huge lifestyle images, banners,
pennants and photomurals set a strong graphic theme. Inside the
arena-shaped shop, a team tower fixture features regional team
apparel. Perimeter walls on risers emphasize boundaries and
highlight mannequin displays and graphics.

◆

Fixturing, signage and mannequins/forms: Mobius, Inc., Eugene, Ore.
Fabrics: Wicklund Design, Long Lake, Minn.

ROCKY SALSKOV, SEATTLE

THE ORIGINAL LEVI'S STORE
NEW YORK CITY

Bergmeyer Associates, Inc., Boston — David Tubridy, president; Joseph Nevin, principal-in-charge; Daniel Broggi, project manager; Christine Canning, interiors; Kelly Ryan, Jamie Lee, Scott Burke and Brian Anderson, project team.

The Original Levi's Store team: Tim Sullivan, director of visual merchandising; Susan Shepherd, regional manager; Kip Saucier, visual merchandising; Beth Barry, general manager.

◆

For Levi's new flagship location, the designers wanted to create a state-of-the-art, multi-media environment. A stainless steel and granite facade allows maximum exposure of the inside. An atrium unifies the store's four floors with monumental stainless steel stairs and an elevator. Flooring consists of Scandinavian beechwood with inlaid red strips and granite tile walkways. Red slab walls are a trademark reference to Levi's internationally recognized red tab. Eight interactive kiosk directories (available in English, French, German and Spanish) on the ground level are designed to assist customer's navigation of the store.

◆

Lighting design: Ripman Lighting, Belmont, Mass., Chris Ripman and Adam Kibbe, Architect: Bergmeyer Associates, Inc., Boston; General Contractor: Richter + Ratner, Maspeth, N.Y.; Fixturing: Conrad Co., Avon, Mass.; Flooring: Junckers Wood Flooring, Indianapolis; Lighting: Pyramid Electric, Philadelphia; Signage: Midtown Neon Sign Corp., New York City; Props/decoratives: les beaux Oubrages, Montreal (sculpture manufacturer); Millwork Manufacturer: J.S. MacLean Co., Columbus, Ohio; Hardware Manufacturer: Gilbert Industries, Ltd., St. Laurent, Que.; Audio/video: GAVI Industries, Inc., Valley Stream, N.Y. (systems integrator); Barco Inc./Display Products, Kennesaw, Ga. (video supplier); Stewart Filmscreen Corp., Torrance, Calif. (filmscreen supplier); Crimson Tech, Cambridge, Mass. (interactive kiosk computer supplier); Stair fabricators: SRS, Inc., Metuchen, N.J.

SONY STYLE
MADISON AVENUE, NEW YORK CITY

James Mansour Ltd., New York City: James Mansour, president; Martin Jerry, vice president design, William Koo, visual merchandising director; Manon Zinzell, design manager
Sony team: Harlan Bratcher, vice president retail development; Christine Belich, visual events director; Leigh Ann Tischler, visual events coordinator; Tammy Stubbs, graphics; Robert Erdman, merchandise director; Dave Clare, director production and vendor management; Lisa Welch, manager show coordination

◆

Sophisticated, streamlined fixtures are part of an interior designed to introduce Sony electronics, music and movies to customers. The intention was to highlight the product without making the customer aware of the technical requirements in an entertaining environment.

◆

Architectural consultant: William Commer Associates, Midland Park, N.J.; General contractor: Structure Tone. New York City; Props: Greneker, Los Angeles (window sculptures); Design Solutions, (oversized holiday balls); Fixturing: NJS Carpentry Inc., Union City, N.J.; Furniture: Donghia, New York City; Mannequins: Pucci, New York City Graphics: Duggal, New York City (digital photomural); Flooring: Ventec, Chicago ; Lighting: Derksen Light Technology, Orangevale, Calif.; Interior: Exhibit Corporation of America, (interior holiday installation); Lighting and fiber-optics: Modular, Philadelphia; Painted finishes: Creative Finishes, New York City

"SPORT"
SONY PLAZA
NEW YORK CITY

Sony, New York City — Christine Belich, creative director; LeighAnn Tischler, visual merchandising; Tammy Stubbs, retail graphics

◆

This Sony window was part of a campaign to promote a summer line of personal electronics. The mirrored "lenses" on the people in photographer Hans Neleman's shots reflect images on film placed against the window, but transparent from the viewer's perspective.

◆

Digital imaging and printing: Duggal Creative Imaging, New York City

ROSS MUIR, NEW YORK CITY

"PC BY SONY"
SONY STYLE
NEW YORK CITY

Christine Belich, creative director;
Leigh Ann Tischler, visual events
coordinator; Tammy Stubbs, retail
graphics; Jeanine Gerding, lightbox
designs

◆

Another set of Sony Windows
heralded the launch of the PC by
Sony, employing lenticular
imaging for a 3-D effect. The
windows range from witty to
surreal, as is the case with an
array of barnyard fowl ogling
the new machine. Another
window suggests that the
machine can provide a
wellspring of ideas, symbolized
by lightbulbs above the
mannequin heads in the
foreground. A robot-populated
moonscape playfully positions
the PC as cutting-edge
technology in another window,
while in still another, the PC by
Sony relegates previous
computers to the ash heap of
history.

◆

Graphics: Duggal Creative Imaging,
New York City (3M graphics), Jeanine
Gerding, Marc Turnage and Pete
Silvia. Linticular Images: Kodak
Dynamic Imaging, Rochester, N.Y.,
and Duggal Creative Imaging, New
York City

ARI MESA, BROOKLYN, N.Y.

GUESS
NEWBERRY STREET
BOSTON

Guess, Los Angeles: Graham Luck, vice president of construction; Judith Winchester, former director of visual merchandising; Geert De Turck, former director of architecture. Design consultant: Alain Chenu, Marseilles, France (Hawaii store).

◆

The new Guess prototype on Boston's Newberry Street features warm woods and a rolling library ladder in a floor-to-ceiling denim wall that makes a powerful statement about Guess' core business. The wooden "file cabinet" combines a straightforward feel with wit, and images reminiscent of the retailer's advertising provide backdrops for the display window.

◆

Architect: Gundersun and Associates, Salem, Mass.; General contractor: Hirsch Construction, Salem, Mass.; Fixtures: Chris Fischer Productions, Phoenix; Fusion Specialties, Broomfield, Colo.; Patina-V, City of Industry, Calif.; Furniture and props: Fusion Specialties, Broomfield, Colo.; Domestic, Los Angeles; Design Compendium, Brooklyn, N.Y.; Flooring: Ann Sachs, Los Angeles; Bensson, N. Hollywood, Calif. Finishes: Galice, Los Angeles; Lighting: Mid West Lighting, Los Angeles; Wall paintings: Superior Backings, Los Angeles; Signage: Royal Laser, Ontario; Signart, Dallas; Graphics: Production Photographics, Hawthorn, Calif.; Cies Sexton, Denver; Mannequins and forms: Greneker Mannequins, Los Angeles; Fusion Specialties, Broomfield, Colo.

ANDREW BORDWIN, NEW YORK CITY

58

PERSONAL PAIR STORE
NORTHPARK MALL, DALLAS

Design: Robert G. Lyon & Associates, Inc., Schiller Park, Ill.: Joseph Geoghehan Jr., president; Meg Littrell, designer; Jeff Radtke, client manager

◆

Levi's new Personal Pair Store, where customers order custom jeans, focuses on communicating custom services and individual fit through graphics instead of fixtures and ready-made merchandise. High technology, reflected in the metal surfacing throughout, combines with wood and comfortable furniture.

◆

Fixtures: Woodmasters, Addison, Ill.; Gilbert, St. Laurent, Que.; Lighting: Juno Lighting, Des Plaines, Ill.; Tech Lighting, Chicago. Flooring: Bentley Mills, Inc., Chicago (carpet); Graniti Fiandre, Itasca, Ill. (hard flooring); Ceiling: USG Interiors, Inc., Chicago; Treadway Industries, Leesburg, Fla.; Storefront: Treadway Industries; Drapery: Indecor Contract Window Treatments, Chicago

MICHAEL HOUGHTON, STUDIOHIO, COLUMBUS, OHIO

OSHKOSH B'GOSH
TOWN CENTER PLAZA, LEAWOOD, KANSAS

FRCH Design Worldwide, New York City
OshKosh B'Gosh team: Doug Hyde, president & ceo; Paul Lowry, vice president corporate retail; Seth Lerner, director of real estate; Chuck Hensley, construction manager; Joshua Mast, visual merchandising coordinator

◆

The new OshKosh B'Gosh store, with a train station design inspired by the firm's roots as a maker of overalls for railroad workers, draws on nostalgic appeal. Red stained wood and natural pine create a train-track effect down the center aisle, and the cashwrap resembles a ticket booth complete with railroad whistles mounted on the sides. Children can play in a caboose playhouse in the back of the space, while fixtures are inspired by boxcars and railroad crossing signs.

◆

Wood veneer: Dooge Veneer, West Hartford, Conn.; Fixtures: Precision Fixtures & Graphics, Largo, Fla.; Carpet: Atlas Carpet, Long Island City, N.Y.; Clodan Carpets, New York City; Wood flooring: Applied Radiant Energy, Lynchburg, Va.; Plastic laminate: Abet Laminati, Englewood, N.J.; Vinyl base: Johnsonite, Chagrin Falls, Ohio; Vinyl Tile: Azrock, Rutherford, N.J.; Paint: Benjamin Moore, Montvale, N.J.; Light fixtures: Indy Lighting, Fishers, Ind.; Lightron, New Windsor, N.Y.; Spero Lighting, Cleveland; Sign fabricator: Ozark Mountain Interiors, Springfield, Mo.; General contractor: Ozark Mountain Interiors, Springfield, Mo.; Engineer: M-E Engineering, Columbus, Ohio

DOUG METHOD, OLATHE, KAN.

SEASONAL

Holidays and seasonal changes have long offered dramatic opportunities for display. The orchestration of familiar fairy tales and entirely new stories in animation, sculpture and illustration, with lights, music, graphics, rich fabrics and glittering special effects take full advantage of some of the largest presentation budgets of the year. Whether intended solely for entertainment value — as gifts to the local population — or designed to feature merchandise from holiday apparel to gifts, visual techniques make these windows, interiors and public spaces more spectacular each year. ◆ On the large scale, there's projects like Atlanta's Lenox Square, from the exterior laser light show coordinated with local radio station programming to the interior animated sculptures, costumed live characters and Santa's high-backed red throne in a

fantasy of ice. Proving that much of the fun lies in the various interpretations of this familiar setting, at the Deptford Mall in New Jersey, Santa's seat was a comfortable easy chair set in an oversized toyland. ◆ On a smaller scale, New York City's Rockefeller Center filled both vacant windows and those of current tenants with holiday celebrations. Cole-Haan's toy theme poised huge Jack-in-the-boxes against the merchant's shoes and purses. In the center's vacant windows, a parade of carousel animals was constructed of birch twigs on welded metal frames, then strung with tiny colored lights. ◆ Christmas, however, is by no means the only seasonal event to inspire special presentations. In this chapter you'll also find visual merchandising for Valentine's Day, Halloween and other special occasions.

Lenox Square, Atlanta

"GENE MOORE'S ICE FANTASY"
LENOX SQUARE MALL, ATLANTA

The Gene Moore Design Group, New York City: Gene Moore, designer; James Damian, designer/producer/director; Richard Giglio, designer/illustrator.

Lenox Square team: Corporate Property Investors, New York City — Sherry Johnson, director of marketing; David Mack, director of development; Maura Eggan, regional marketing; Lenox Square Merchants Association, Atlanta — Debra Lowry

◆

Part of the major renovation of Lenox Square, a major investment in new holiday decor was intended to establish the center as the premiere shopping experience in the marketplace.

The "Ice Fantasy" brought together a 30-foot grand tree, fantasy animal characters, computerized light show and music, together with large-scale story book (written by Gene Moore) and icicle-hung Georgian garden gazebo for Santa.

◆

Production and project management: Damian-Randd, Skillman, N.J.; Architecture: RTKL, Dallas; Structural engineers: Ellison & Tanner Inc., Dallas; Rigging: Production & Rigging Resources Inc., Dallas; Jerry Gilleland Productions, Atlanta; Lighting design: Ian Knight and John Morgan, Los Angeles; Lighting: Syncrolite Systems, Dallas; Costume design: Alvin Colt, New York City; Fabrication: Mulder Martin Inc., New York City (costumes); Store Decor, Ft. Worth (parachute characters); Studio Productions, Tempe Ariz. (grand tree); Wold & Co., Dallas (Santa's gazebo); JT&L Dallas (exterior steel stars and roof set); Sculptor: Alexsander Denel, New York City (ice fairies and parachute characters); Ice fairy costumer: Winn Morton, Dallas; Ice fairy animator: Jim Elliott, Dallas; Iced Fountain Set: DS Arts, Dallas; Music/exterior show: James Neel Music House, Dallas; Music/interior show: Graebar Studios, New York City

JOHN WADSWORTH, NORFOLK, VA.

"A VISIT FROM ST. NICHOLAS"
LORD & TAYLOR
NEW YORK CITY

Bill Conard, window director; Manoel Renha, art director; Loren Dunham, fashion coordinator; Frank Reilly, Doug Fowler, Chris Stoeckel, window display team; Alan Petersen, vice president of visual merchandising

◆

In a series of six ten-foot-high windows, Clement C. Moore's familiar poem was told through animation, painted backdrops and thirty sculptured and costumed figures. Painted backdrops were styled to resemble vintage post cards and based on the pen-and-ink illustrations of Thomas Nast. The script of the poem, accompanying each window scene, was reproduced from the author's own handwritten script.

◆

Construction/fabrication: Spaeth Design, New York City

GERALD MALON, SPOTSWOOD, N.J.

"ACCESSORIES — CHRISTMAS"
LORD & TAYLOR
NEW YORK CITY

Alan Petersen, vice president of visual merchandising; Manoel Renha, creative director for visual and windows; Frank Reilly, lights/production; Doug Fowler, productio n

◆

Enlarged photographs of featured products provided the basic building blocks for Lord & Taylor's accessories window during the 1995 Christmas season. The Lord & Taylor design team mounted enlarged photos of handbags, sunglasses and other accessories on double-weight illustration board, then trimmed them to fit the cubes that were used as pedestals for the real merchandise.

◆

Ceilings: Gleason Paints, Woodside, N.Y.; Flooring: Dykes Lumber; Wall coverings and fabrics: Circle Fabrics, New York City; Signage: Electra Communications, Islandia, N.Y.; Graphics: Time/Life Photo Laboratories

GERALD MALON, SPOTSWOOD, N.J.

"IMAGINATION CENTRAL"
DEPTFORD MALL
DEPTFORD, N.J.

The Becker Group, Baltimore, Md. —
Glenn Tilley, senior account executive;
Ken Hobart, creative director; Jane
Eichler, project manager
Store team: Mark Letendre, marketing
director, Deptford Mall

◆

Focusing on flight and fantasy as
its holiday theme, overhead
decor included a 15-foot
simulated hot-air balloon and a
variety of flying machines. The
central 36-foot tree was crowned
with a whimsical weathervane.
Animated elves were at work in
a toy-factory of turning gears
and cranes. Santa, located inside
the tree, was surrounded by a
high-tech power generator and
control panel.

◆

Fabrication: The Becker Group,
Baltimore, Md.

MARK WIELAND, WASHINGTON, D.C.

"HOLIDAY WINDOWS"
ROCKEFELLER CENTER
NEW YORK CITY

Julin & Larrabee Designs, New York City — Scott Larrabee and David Julin,
visual merchandise directors; Kemie Yonnayama, Saho Stewart, Jeffery
Papile, Jin Sook Han, Francisco Rueda, Eddie Calcagon, Hsio-ning Tu and
Paul Paddock, design team

◆

To enliven vacant windows in a Rockefeller Center space formerly
occupied by a bank tenant, the Julin & Larrabee design team
constructed a menagerie of carousel animals of birch twigs on
welded metal frames. Fabric, ribbons and lights decorated the
animal forms, which ranged from fish and fowl to mammals
including camel, a rabbit and horses.

◆

Fabrics: Circle Fabrics, New York City;
Props/sculptures: Jeffery Mase, New York City

"RUSSIAN FANTASY"
STANLEY KORSHAK
CRESCENT COURT, DALLAS

Rajan Patel, fashion director, visual;
Jeffrey Marion Lee, visual director

◆

Taking inspiration from Faberge
and the work of Russian master
goldsmiths, the Stanley Korshak
design team created storewide
displays based on their motifs,
patterns and colors. The
storefront display featured a
cement pillar and wrought-iron
gate facade, a gold-leaf carriage
and a celosia horse. In the
store's two front windows,
Faberge eggs were carved out to
showcase merchandise.
Mannequin platforms were
staged as miniature garden
scenes, with jeweled insects
lighting on topiary forms.

◆

Suppliers: Cascade Foam, Dallas;
Christine Taylor, Doylestown, Pa.;
Adel Rootstein, New York City
(mannequins); Montage Images,
Dallas; Presentations Plus, Long Lake,
Minn.; Coburn Plastics,
Lakewood, N.J.

74

MICHAEL MANUEL, DALLAS

SEASON OF CELEBRATIO

"A SEASON OF CELEBRATION"
ZCMI, ZCMI CENTER
SALT LAKE CITY

Mike Stephens, visual director; Dennis Wardle, design; Lighting design: Peter
Willardson, Salt Lake City

◆

Celebrating Utah's centennial, ZCMI posed an elegantly
appareled mannequin against rich holiday colors and surfaces.
Quilted green hangings contrast with the bright red of potted
amaryllis; and a multitude of shimmering gold and pearl-colored
Christmas balls ornament an oversized wreath above an antique
table.

◆

Mannequins: Adel Rootstein, New York City; Props/decoratives: Whitehurst
Imports, San Francisco; Fabrics: Visual Fabrics, Winsted, Conn.; Lighting:
Halo, Elk Grove Village, Ill.; Flooring: Ottley, Salt Lake City

DENNIS POTTS, SALT LAKE CITY

"SYMPHONY BALL"
ZCMI, SALT LAKE CITY

Mike Stephens, visual director; Celeste Cecchini, designer

◆

For the past two years, ZCMI has sponsored a New Year's Eve ball
to benefit the local symphony orchestra. To promote ticket sales for
the event, as well as the sale of formal evening attire, the retailer
set up a display outside of the designer dress department on the
main aisle. In windows, wire spheres were sprayed gloss black
and dabbed with gold leaf. A ten-foot gold-leafed tabled adds a
horizontal shape.

◆

Mannequins: Adel Rootstein Inc., New York City Props: George Dell, New
York City; Signage: ZCMI, Salt Lake City; Lighting: Halo Lighting, Elk Grove
Village, Ill.

"PETER PAN"
ZCMI, ACMI CENTER
SALT LAKE CITY

Mike Stephens, visual director; Tim Davis, designer

◆

Larger-than-life photographs of the four main characters promote
Ballet West's production of Peter Pan. The trunk of the tree and the
oversized mushrooms were sculpted of papier-mache; sheer fabric,
torn and dyed green, suggests the canopy of trees. Mylar on the
floor creates the effect of water.

◆

Lighting: Halo Lighting, Elk Grove Village, Ill.; Signage: ZCMI, Salt Lake City;
Graphics: Ballet West, Salt Lake City

DENNIS POTTS, SALT LAKE CITY

"DREAMKEEPERS"
ZCMI, SALT LAKE CITY

Mike Stephens, visual director; Dennis Wardle, designer

◆

Recreated backdrops of original set designs were painted on
suspended canvases to announce the world premiere of the Utah
Opera's production of "Dreamkeepers."

◆

Lighting: Halo Lighting, Elk Grove Village, Ill.; Fabrics: Silver State, Salt Lake
City; Signage: ZCMI, Salt Lake City; Graphics: Utah Opera, Michael Downs,
Salt Lake City

F.A.O. SCHWARZ BEAR
THE WESTCHESTER MALL
WHITE PLAINS, N.Y.

The Becker Group, Baltimore:
Gordon Becker, president, senior account executive; Sarah Mudge,
account executive; Sinclair Russell,
creative director; Tim Boulay, project
coordinator; Anica Archip,
marketing director at The Westchester Mall

◆

A 24-foot-tall inflatable bronze-
and-gold-lamé bear,
surrounded by oversized gift
boxes and giant F.A.O.
signature letter blocks, is an
exact replica of the famous toy
store's trademark. Overhead
decor included 15-foot-tall
inflated cold-air balloons
suspended from the ceiling
throughout the center, outlined
in mini-lights, festooned with
gold lamé ribbons and bows
and containing teddy bears and
gifts.

◆

Fabrication: The Becker Group,
Baltimore

"SEEING STARS"
PAUL STUART
MADISON AVENUE, NEW YORK CITY
NORTH MICHIGAN AVENUE, CHICAGO

Tom Beebe, creative director; Elaine Argiro, advertising director; Mona Reilly, public relations director; New York design team: Gerry Fredella and Michael Verbert, co-visual managers; Chicago design team: Catia Marchetti, visual manager; Joel Boechman and Jeff Mills, visual assistants

◆

As a way to interpret the magic of Christmas without using traditional wreaths and garlands, the Paul Stuart design team made stars the focal point of holiday windows at the New York City and Chicago stores. Political satirist Geoffrey Moss gave the stars faces, bodies and personalities. Paul Stuart dedicated one store window to the Starlight Foundation, a non-profit organization that grants wishes and provides entertainment to critically, chronically or terminally ill children.

◆

Artist: Geoffrey Moss, New York City (star faces); New York suppliers: Mark Backman, Great Barrington, Mass. (scenic artist, stars and other props); Gilbey Graphics, New York City (graphics); Encore/Eclectic, New York City (props); Trengrove, New York City (icicles and splashes); In Costume, New York City (Santa suit); Santa's World, New York City (crystal star ornaments and star boxes); Aromatique, Herbert Springs, Ark. (potpourri)
Chicago suppliers: Signature Screen Printing, Chicago (graphics); Prop Room, Chicago (props); Chicago Riverfront Antique Mart, Chicago (props); Evergreen Specialty Co., Denver (interior wreaths and garland)

ARI MESA, NEW YORK CITY

"JACK-IN-THE-BOX WINDOWS"
COLE-HAAN
NEW YORK CITY

Elena Petrocco and Judy Hamlin,
visual merchandising directors

◆

Cole-Haan's holiday windows
sprung into the season with the
help of the traditional jack-in-the-
box. Whether singing a
Christmas carol or springing
under the mistletoe, the popular
toy of Christmases past drew
attention to featured handbags
and purses at the Rockefeller
Avenue store.

◆

Project artists: Tony Pellegrino, Toni
Wolf and Michael Reidy, New York
City; Design assistance: Julin &
Larrabee Designs, New York City

"FAIRY TALE UNDER GLASS"
FORTUNOFF
NEW YORK CITY

Peter Moodie, design director;
Ellen Rixford Studio, New York City —
Ellen Rixford, project director;
Mayhew Lu and Ellen Rixford, design
team

◆

Holiday windows for the new
Fortunoff, New York City, spun a
fairy tale of a king's gifts to his
family. In the animated window
displays, the queen receives her
gift of jewelry while the princess
receives a dancing fairy. Life-
sized human figures were made
of stocking material over polyfil
and cotton batting on structures
of padded wire and carved
foam. The jointed, wooden fairy
was motorized, and a motorized
wizard swings a wand
decorated with miniature
twinkling lights.

◆

Fabrication: Ellen Rixford Studio, New
York City

ELLEN RIXFORD STUDIO, NEW YORK CITY

86

"THE NIGHT BEFORE CHRISTMAS"
O.C. TANNER
SALT LAKE CITY

Brent Erkelens, visual merchandising director/designer; Jeri Wiscomb, Michele Lund, Carolyn Barrett, Rick Ith, Megan Ith, Evelyn Erkelens, Virginia Wallin and Rosie Burbidge, project team

◆

O.C. Tanner's holiday presentation featured 12 puppet theater sets with marionettes acting out the famous Christmas Eve poem and corresponding text appearing at the bottom of each set. The first window ("....not a creature was stirring...") featured a giant mouse sleeping on a living room sofa, with mouse traps scattered around the floor. The intricate theater sets included puppets dressed in silks, suedes and furs, flickering fires and candles, miniature hand-made quilts and other details scaled to the marionettes' size.

◆

Marionettes: Bob Barker Marionettes, Los Angeles

DENNIS POTTS, SALT LAKE CITY

"HOLIDAY WINDOWS"
MACY'S
NEW YORK CITY

Sam Joseph, window director;
Brett Horne, project manager.
Macy's windows staff

◆

Focusing on a "World's Most
Exciting Show" theme, the
Macy's design team created a
circus setting complete with
"performing" seals and other
exotic animals, a Christmas-
oriented "freak show" with a
double-headed reindeer and a
traditional fun house. All
windows integrated
merchandise with the circus
theme and many featured tent-
like fabric treatments to help set
the stage.

◆

Props/decoratives/mannequins/
forms: Creative Arts Unlimited,
Pinellas Park, Fla.

ARI MESA, BAYSIDE, N.Y.

"SONY STYLE"
MADISON AVENUE, NEW YORK CITY

James Mansour Ltd., New York City:
James Mansour, president; William
Koo, visual merchandising director;
Manon Zinzell, design manager
Sony Team: Christine Belich, visual
events director; Leigh Ann Tischler,
visual events coordinator

◆

Giant-sized Christmas ball
ornaments dominate the
electronics merchandise.
In a series of six lifestyle
windows, each 19-foot-tall
window featured bits of legs and
hands, overscaled so that a
complete figure would stand 12
feet tall. Customers lifestyles
parodied in the windows ranged
from rap artist — with Tommy
Hilfiger knapsack, Timberland
boots and Tag Huer watch — to
"the ladies who lunch," with
Chanel pumps, handbags and
pearls. Featured entertainment
and electronics merchandise was
also oversized.

◆

Props: Greneker, Los Angeles
(window sculptures); Design
Solutions, (oversized holiday balls)
Fixturing: NJS Carpentry Inc., Union
City, N.J. Furniture: Donghia, New
York City Mannequins: Pucci, New
York City Graphics: Duggal, New
York City (digital photomural)
Flooring: Ventec, Chicago Lighting:
Derksen Light Technology, Orange-
vale, Calif. Interior: Exhibit
Corporation of America, (interior
holiday installation) Lighting and
fiberoptics: Modular, Philadelphia
PaintED Finishes: Creative Finishes,
New York City

"SONY STYLE"
MADISON AVENUE,
NEW YORK CITY

"FLOWERING FIELD'S"

MARSHALL FIELD'S STATE STREET, CHICAGO

Steve Didier, window display manager; Amy Meadows, visual merchandising manager (State Street); Ann Greenstein, designer; Jamie Becker, director of visual merchandising; Andrew Markopoulos, senior vice president of visual merchandising and design (retired), Dayton-Hudson Department Stores, Minneapolis

◆

Augmented with platforms and cornucopia, the classical architecture of the Chicago flagship store offered customers a city block's worth of shopping among landscaped gardens. Thirteen display windows presented stylized art history lessons, each devoted to a different artist-inspired fantasy garden. Floral and visual designers worked together closely in the development of these presentations, with garden gazing globes, weathervanes and sundials designed for each window in the style of the artist.

◆

Interscaping: S.F. Productions, San Francisco; Flowers: Podesta and Baldocchi, San Francisco; Props: Silvestri of California, Los Angeles (framed pieces and garden sculptures; Backdrops and prop painting: KINC, Chicago

SUSAN KEZON, CHICAGO

94

Flowering Field's
Marshall Field's Second Annual Flower Show

"MUSIC BOXES"
ZCMI,
ZCMI CENTER,
SALT LAKE CITY

Mike Stephens, visual director;
Richard H. Madsen, president/ceo

◆

The ZCMI design team created
and dedicated a series of custom
music boxes in the store's
holiday windows to Utah's
Centennial Celebration. The
ornate music boxes were
entitled, "Beesness as Usual,"
"Happy Birthday Utah,"
"Essence of the Lake," "Diva,"
and "Peace."

◆

Music box designers: Sherri Orton,
Salt Lake City ("Beesness as Usual");
Celeste Cecchini, Salt Lake City
("Happy Birthday Utah"); Tim Davis,
Salt Lake City ("Essence of the
Lake"); Anne Cook, Salt Lake City
("Diva"); Diane Call, Salt Lake City
("Peace"); Lighting designer: Peter
Willardson, Salt Lake City; Lighting:
Halo Lighting, Elk Grove Village, Ill.;
Props/decoratives: Marko
Styrofoam Products, Salt Lake City;
The Beadery, Hope Valley, R.I.;
Cadillac Plastics, Salt Lake City;
Ensign Wholesale Florist, Salt Lake
City; Green's Welding, Salt Lake City

DENNIS POTTS, SALT LAKE CITY

98

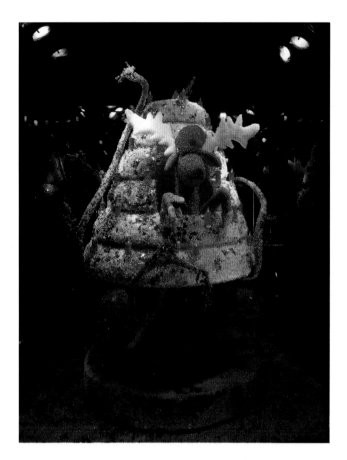

"BRIGHT IDEAS FOR VALENTINE'S"
ZCMI, SALT LAKE CITY

Mike Stephens, visual director; Sherri Orton, designer

◆

Heart-shaped lamps illuminate the candy that ZCMI recommended in this Valentine's Day display.

◆

Suppliers: Halo Lighting, Elk Grove Village, Ill.; International Furniture/Michael Stensgaard, San Francisco

DENNIS POTTS, SALT LAKE CITY

"HALLOWEEN"
ZCMI, SALT LAKE CITY

Mike Stephens, visual director;
Sherri Orton, designer

◆

Electric candelabra take to the
skies amidst levitating candy
bars in this ZCMI Halloween
display. Lighting filtered
through backdrop fabric
creates interesting shadows of
the identifying signage.

◆

Suppliers: Halo Lighting, Elk Grove
Village, Ill.; George Dell, New York
City; Visual Fabrics, Winsted, Utah

DENNIS POTTS, SALT LAKE CITY

"CITY SWEETS"
ZCMI, SALT LAKE CITY

Mike Stephens, visual director;
Debbie Warren, designer

◆

Brownstone "window boxes"
filled with candies make the
visual pun to promote ZCMI's
"City Sweets" department.

◆

Lighting: Halo Lighting, Elk Grove
Village, Ill.

OPPOSITE:

"GARDEN TOYS"
ZCMI, SALT LAKE CITY

Mike Stephens, visual director;
Debbie Warren, designer; Dave
Paxton and Oscar Juarez, project
team

◆

Cauliflower, cabbage and kid
stuff combine in this ZCMI
window promoting garden toys
for the green-thumbed young.

◆

Suppliers: Halo Lighting, Elk Grove
Village, Ill.; Super-Silk, Salt Lake City

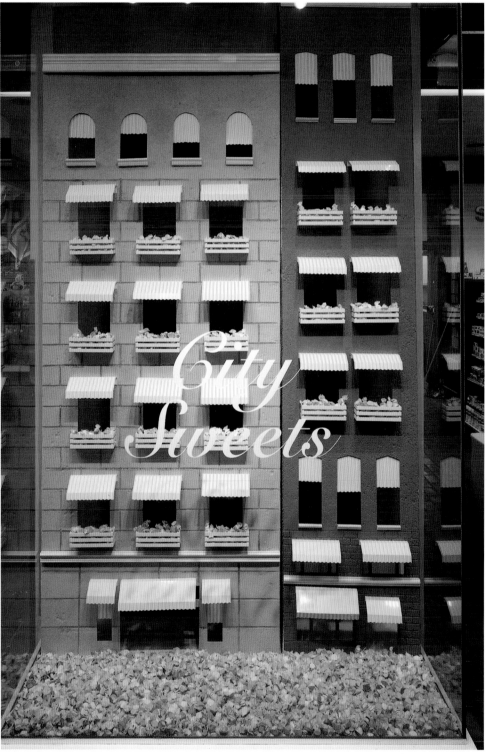

DENNIS POTTS, SALT LAKE CITY

GARDEN • TOYS

APPAREL

While apparel presentation themes run the gamut, this chapter proves beyond a doubt that the best rely on simplicity, clarity and style to communicate their message. In many cases, this means no more than one or two mannequins presenting the merchandise against an interesting backdrop, well lit and identified by concise signage. ◆ You'll see in-store presentations that communicate the retailer's own style while portraying featured apparel and accessory lines — grouped mannequins appareled in workday casual clothing at Marshall Field's; a careful balance of hung, folded and faced-out garments, together with lifestyle graphics, on a modular wall system at Britches in Washington, D.C.; Victoria's Secret's intimate apparel set against fuchsia-colored walls and soft, fabric-draped surfaces; and, at Liz Claiborne in New York City, dresses positioned before a backdrop of modern furniture and glass art pieces. ◆ In windows, innovative apparel displays are themed around everything from natural riverbeds (at ZCMI) to frogs (at Lord & Taylor). High-tech pipe fittings, old-fashioned school desks, gumdrops and origami also make spectacular appearances as props. You'll see the human figure frequently in this chapter — apparel presented to its best on a wide variety of mannequins, forms and shaped hangers — with heads ranging from the realistic through to the abstract and the clearly fantastic, including round metal topiary forms and models of city buildings.

Men's Formal Shop, Saks Fifth Avenue, Beverly Hills, Calif.

MEN'S FORMAL SHOP
SAKS FIFTH AVENUE
BEVERLY HILLS, CALIF.

William Viets, vice president visual merchandising; Poppy Burns, manager
special projects; Gary Fusfeld, Sal Lenzo, Michael Salinas, Anthony
Lombardi, Alfonso Sauceda and Ward Garee, New York visual team;
Michael Bewley and Jac Measley, Beverly Hills visual team

◆

Existing architectural elements in what had been a Chanel boutique
were enhanced with a grand chandelier and furniture to create a
"Hollywood sound stage" regency revival interior compatible with
men's apparel. The chandelier was a flea-market find; existing
loose floor fixtures were removed with the exception of the
caseline and existing single-hung wall hardware. Pique-covered
panels provide a backdrop for a "gallery" of evening shirts and
accessories; stock is housed in an adjacent stockroom.

◆

Mannequins: Pucci, New York City; Superior, New York City (suit forms);
Bernstein, New York City (shirt forms) Mirror: Spartan West, Los Angeles

BRITCHES
WASHINGTON, D.C.

Fisher Gordon Architects, Washington, D.C. — Craig Fisher and George
Gordon, partners; C. Doug Grenade, project manager.
Fixture design: Mathias Thorner Design, Inc. — Mathias Thorner, president;
Bill Chipp, project manager
Britches Great Outdoors, Washington, D.C. — Chet Obieleski, chief financial
officer; Eugene Killway, store planning

◆

A departure from the retailer's existing image, a new wall fixturing
system support restructuring of merchandise departments into
three separate zones. Consisting of waxed, raw steel pipes and
lacquered plywood shelving, the system divides the 14-foot-high
walls into sections. From eye level to floor level, merchandise is
presented in folded and hung presentations. Above, lifestyle
graphics and forms pull together apparel pieces into a coherent
collection.

◆

Fixtures: Hill Enterprises, Gaithersburg, Md.

108

VICTORIA'S SECRET
NORTH MICHIGAN AVENUE
CHICAGO

Limited Store Planning, Columbus, Ohio — Charles Hinson, president; Debbie Urton, vice president design development; Tom Laporte, senior director Intimate Brands Group; Bruce Fithian, design manager; Intimate Brands Group; James Nauyok, presentation development manager; Gilberto Albuquerque, design development manager

◆

Introducing a more daring, colorful image for Victoria's Secret, this unit on North Michigan Avenue was intended to attract a younger clientele. The heart-and-rose motif that begins on the store's facade is carried through interior in signage and graphics, floral arrangement, wallpaper and architectural details.

◆

Architect: Retail Design Group, Columbus, Ohio; General contractor: Capitol Construction, Wheeling, Ill.; Fixturing: Ontario Store Fixtures, Toronto; Furniture: Interior Crafts, Chicago; Flooring: Bentley Mills, Chicago; Lighting: Halo Lighting, Elk Grove Village, Ill.; Signage: North American Signs, South Bend, Ind.; Props/ decoratives: Fusion Inc., Broomfield, Colo.; Greneker, Los Angeles

ANTOINE BOOTZ, NEW YORK CITY

"SWIMWEAR ON 6"
LORD & TAYLOR
FIFTH AVENUE
NEW YORK CITY

William Conard, visual merchandising director (former); Manoel Renha, art director; Loren Dunham, fashion coordinator; Chris Stoeckel, fashion stylist; Doug Fowler, production/sculpture; Frank Reilly, lighting

◆

For a Juniors' swimwear promotion, Lord & Taylor's design team chose frogs as a theme. The large images are painted on canvas; the smaller three-dimensional frogs are clay, hand-molded and painted by the L&T design team.

◆

Mannequins: Adel Rootstein, London and New York City

Swimwear on 6

"OBJECTS OF DESIRE"

MARSHALL FIELD'S STATE STREET, CHICAGO

Steve Didier, window display manager; Amy Meadows, visual merchandising manager (State Street); Jamie Becker, director of visual merchandising; Andrew Markopoulos, senior vice president of visual merchandising and design (retired), Dayton-Hudson Department Stores; Ann Greenstein, Bonnie Nolan, Patrick Ewing, Kevin Grace, State Street window display staff

◆

Clean, linear presentation gives these mannequins a lift on a seemingly floating mirrored platform. Industrial hardware and thick rubber shock cord actually pull this presentation off the floor. A reflected pool of metallic mica-like shards balances the angle of the suspension cords on the floor.

◆

Mannequins: Adel Rootstein, London and New York City

MICHAEL MCCAFREY, CHICAGO

111

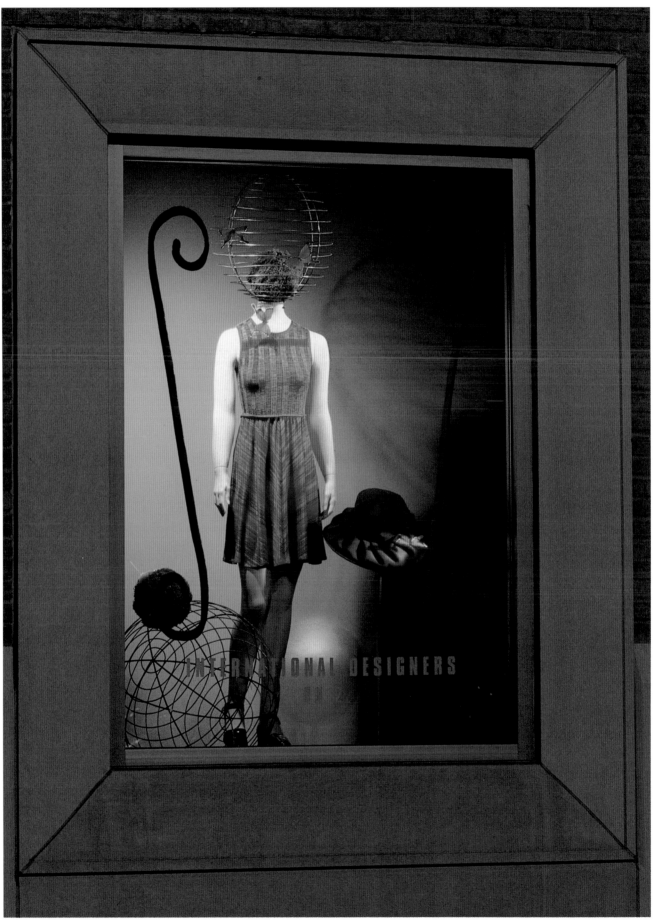

"SPRING 1996"
JACOBSON'S
TOWN CENTER PLAZA
LEAWOOD, KAN.

Gregory P. Digue, visual merchandising manager; Roger Soper, Dee Monts,
Julie Mach, Jeff Bodenhamer and Lisa Kay Shively, project team

◆

The windows at the opening of a new Jacobson's store in
Leawood, Kan., reinforced the idea of fashion as art, placing
dramatically lit mannequins in frames, turning each tableau into an
individual "picture." Spring hats, topiary forms and butterflies add
a seasonal note.

◆

Suppliers: George Dell Inc., New York City; Greneker, Los Angeles;
Stuppy's, Kansas City, Mo. (floral supplies)

WHITNEY COX, NEW YORK CITY

"ARTISTIC ENDEAVORS"
LIZ CLAIBORNE
NEW YORK CITY

The look is residential and loftlike at this Liz Claiborne store. Pale wood flooring and winter white walls create a spacious stage for the couture.

◆

Beyer Blinder Belle, New York City: Fred Bland, partner; Margaret Kittinger, director of interiors and designer in charge; Donald Recchia, Tom Lindberg and Christina Sum, project team.
Liz Claiborne Inc., New York City: Jim Metscher, president of retail division; D. Bradley Lenz, vice president of operations and construction; Wade Petty, director of construction

◆

General contractor: Herbert Construction, New York City; Lighting design: Quentin Thomas Associates Inc., Douglaston, N.Y. — Quentin Thomas, principal; Lighting fixtures: Zumtobel Lighting Inc., Garfield, N.J.; Staff Lighting Corp., Highland, N.Y.; Modular Int'l., Pittsburgh; Indy Lighting Inc., Indianapolis; Custom fixturing: National Store Fixtures & Displays, Pompano Beach, Fla.; J.R. Wire & Metal, Winnipeg, Manitoba; Chris Bundy, New York City; Furniture: Dakota Jackson, Long Island City, N.Y.; Palazzetti Inc., New York City; Cassina USA Inc., Huntington Station, N.Y.; Casa Nova, New York City; Flooring: Prince Street, New York City (antique carpets); Pritcher, Liverpool, N.Y. (wood flooring; Wall coverings: Maharam, New York City; Fabrics: Design Tex Fabrics Inc., Woodside, N.Y.; Pollack, New York City; Crosby Mc Neil, New York City; Hines, New York City; Mannequins and forms: J.R. Wire, Winnipeg, Manitoba; Cable display system: B & N Industries, Inc., San Carlos, Calif.; Framed pictures: Brian Ready, Stamford, Conn.

"DESIGNS WE LIVE IN"
MITCHELL'S OF WESTPORT, WESTPORT, CONN.

Working with local interior designers from the American Society of Interior Designers, Mitchell's created a series of eight windows featuring designer apparel in residential settings. Materials in the windows, including backdrops, props and furniture, were provided for each window by the interior designer who was identified in signage. An in-store reception officially launched the windows and provided customers a chance to meet the designers.

David Cote, display director, Laura Murphy, Seth Orkland, project team

◆

Architect: Beyer Blinder Belle, New York City — Margaret Kittinger, director of interiors and associate partner; General contractor: Herbert Construction, New York City — Keith Kapps, project supervisor; Mechanical, electrical and plumbing: IR&R, New York City   Ken Zuar, partner in charge of HVAC; Lighting design: Quentin Thomas Associates Inc., Douglaston, N.Y. — Quentin Thomas, principal; Lighting fixtures: Zumtobel Lighting Inc., Garfield, N.J.; Staff Lighting Corp., Highland, N.Y.,

Modular Int'l., Pittsburgh; Indy Lighting Inc., Indianapolis; Custom fixturing: National Store Fixtures & Displays, Pompano Beach, Fla.; J.R. Wire & Metal, Winnipeg, Manitoba; Chris Bundy, New York City; Furniture: Dakota Jackson, Long Island City, N.Y.; Palazzetti Inc., New York City; Cassina USA Inc., Huntington Station, N.Y.; Casa Nova, New York City; Flooring: Prince Street, New York City (antique carpets), Pritcher, Liverpool, N.Y. (wood flooring; Wall coverings: Maharam, New York City; Fabrics: Design Tex Fabrics Inc., Woodside, N.Y.; Pollack, New York City; Crosby Mc Neil, New York City; Hines, New York City; Mannequins and forms:

J.R. Wire, Winnipeg, Manitoba; Cable display system: B & N Industries, Inc., San Carlos, Calif.; Framed pictures: Brian Ready, Stamford, Conn.

ADRIANNE DEPOLO, ROWAYTON, CONN.

VITRASHOP
EUROSHOP '96, DUSSELDORF GERMANY

James Mansour Ltd., New York City: James Mansour, president; William Koo, visual merchandising director; Manon Zinzell, design manager Vitrashop team: Ursula Rohrer and Peter Fuchs

◆

The 10,000 square feet exhibit of Swiss-based Vitrashop's fixtures was conceived as a series of departments within a mythical store. Graphics coordinate with the company's catalogs, and the lighting, props and merchandise presentation were arranged to look as much like an actual store as possible.

◆

Wall coverings: Maya Romanoff, Chicago; Projectors: Derksen Lighting Technology, Orangevale, Calif.; Props: Greneker, Los Angeles; Permanent Foliage, New York City (floral arrangement); Video: Electrosonic, Minneapolis (video); Music: AEI, Seattle (music); Forms: Fusion Specialties, Broomfield, Colo. (dressmaker forms); Photomurals: Cies Sexton, Denver; Furniture: Vitrashop, Basel, Switzerland

A GERHARDT, BOETZINGEN, GERMANY
H.G. ESCH, COLOGNE, GERMANY

A GERHARDT, BOETZINGEN, GERMANY
H.G. ESCH, COLOGNE, GERMANY

"SCHOOL ZONE"
ZCMI, SALT LAKE CITY

Mike Stephens, visual director; Celeste Toigo Cecchini, designer

◆

This back-to-school presentation places child mannequins on tiers of brightly colored chairs and desks. School textbooks cover the floor.

◆

Suppliers: Halo Lighting, Elk Grove Village, Ill.; Adel Rootstein, New York City; The Family Store, Pocatello, Utah

"ANNE KLEIN & CO."
ZCMI, SALT LAKE CITY

Mike Stephens, visual director;
Diane Call, designer

◆

Fashions from Anne Klein are
shown at ZCMI against a wall of
brown, gold and silver
corrugated triangles. Amber cut-
glass tiles were glued in the
center of each square in a grid
pattern on the back wall.

◆

Suppliers: Halo Lighting, Elk Grove
Village, Ill.; Adel Rootstein, New York
City; Dixon Paper, Salt Lake City;
Oasis Stage Works, Salt Lake City

DENNIS POTTS, SALT LAKE CITY

"MICHAEL KORS"
MARSHALL FIELD'S
STATE STREET, CHICAGO

Steve Didier, window display manager; Amy Meadows, visual merchandising manager (State Street); Jamie Becker, director of visual merchandising; Andrew Markopoulos, senior vice president of visual merchandising and design (retired), Dayton-Hudson Department Stores, Minneapolis; Ann Greenstein, Patrick Ewing, Bonnie Nolan, Kevin Grace and Cesar Jacinto, State Street window display team

◆

This presentation of Michael Kors fashions relies on the power of neon against curved, frosted panels. Hi-tech metal poles, clamps and coils further the futuristic theme.

◆

Auto-pole system: ALU, New York City; Frosted Plexiglass® panels: Niedermaier, Chicago; Mannequins: Adel Rootstein, New York City; Neon: Neon Design, Chicago

MICHAEL KORS

MICHAEL MCCAFREY, CHICAGO

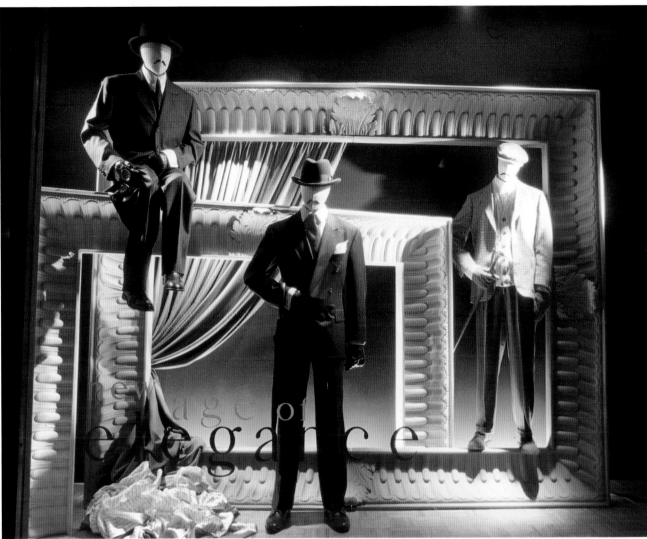

MICHAEL MCCAFREY, CHICAGO

"THE NEW AGE OF ELEGANCE"
MARSHALL FIELD'S
STATE STREET, CHICAGO

Steve Didier, window display manager; Amy Meadows, visual merchandising
manager (State Street); Jamie Becker, director of visual merchandising; Andrew
Markopoulos, senior vice president of visual merchandising and design, (retired)
Dayton-Hudson Department Stores, Minneapolis; Ann Greenstein, Patrick Ewing,
Bonnie Nolan, Kevin Grace and Cesar Jacinto, State Street window display team

✦

The "New Age of Elegance" — a fall fashion display — used molding to
construct supersized picture frames that give riser height to mannequin
groupings. The strong back lighting and whimsical mustached
mannequins complete a picture of elegant menswear.

◆

Oversized frame pieces: Silvestri of California, Los Angeles; Mannequins:
Bernstein Displays, Astoria, N.Y.

ON 2

"SALUTE TO L.A."
SAKS FIFTH AVENUE
NEW YORK CITY

William J. Viets, vice president visual merchandising; Gary Fusfield, Anthony
Lombardi, Sal Lenzo, Michael Salinas, Alfonso Sauceda, Ward Garee, Poppy
Burns, B.H. Michael Bewley and Jac Measley, project team

◆

This "Salute to L.A." at the Beverly Hills Saks Fifth Avenue uses a
backdrop that combines the look of a freeway and a spool of film to
frame mannequins with L.A. totems on their minds.

◆

Mannequins: Hindsgaul, New York City; Masks: Discoveries, Long Island City, N.Y.

THIERRY MUGLER ON 3

"EXPLORATION OF BLACK AND WHITE"
BEACHWOOD PLACE
BEACHWOOD, OHIO

J.M.A. Productions, Chardon, Ohio: John Simoneau, artistic director; Jill
Griffith, Mike Anderson and Dave Callahan, visual merchandising team

◆

It's a black-and-white world in this JMA display (with the
occasional purple-haired accent). It's proof that even the most
limited palette can be arresting.

◆

Windmill, furniture, hairpieces, jewelry and accessories: J.M.A. Productions,
Chardon, Ohio

DAN ELGHAYAN, CLEVELAND

"FASHION AMONG THE STARS"
BEACHWOOD PLACE
BEACHWOOD, OHIO

J.M.A. Productions, Chardon, Ohio: John Simoneau, artistic director; Violet
Ferritto, Mike Anderson and Dave Callahan, visual merchandising team

◆

This display, dubbed "Fashion Among the Stars," energizes the
display floor with bold colors and aggressive shapes.

◆

Furniture, props and staging: J.M.A. Productions, Chardon, Ohio; Fabric:
Cutting Room Fabrics; Balloons: Balloon Crew, Berea, Ohio

ANN TAYLOR LOFT
RIVERHEAD, N.Y.

Desgrippes Gobe & Associates, New York City: Marc Gobe,
principal; Wendy Hald, creative director; Mary Meuer, design
director and project manager; Victoria Kirk, designer

◆

Intended to appeal to young women beginning their careers, the
outlet store features simple, functional fixtures and a warehouse-
turned-residence atmosphere. Brushed nickel, particleboard and
maple-trimmed display racks divide the 12,500-square-foot store
into separate merchandise areas.

◆

Architect: Park/Retail Design, New York City; Fixtures: Ontario Store Fixtures
Inc., Weston, Ont.; Flooring: Gerbert Limited, Lancaster, Pa. (vinyl floor tiles);
Architectural Systems Inc., New York City (hardwood floor)

TODAY'S MAN
FIFTH AVENUE, NEW YORK CITY

James Mansour Ltd., New York City: James Mansour, president; William Koo, visual merchandising director; Manon Zinzell, design manager; Mindy Gurwicz, Today's Man visual merchandising manager

◆

In order to create focal points in the very large store, visuals focused on presenting head-to-toe merchandise statements to define each department. Forms and figures are used generously throughout the space, supported by lifestyle photography. Mission, style and customer service statements are communicated on etched glass panels mounted to columns in each area of the store.

◆

Signage: Big Apple Sign, New York City; Casework: Beacon Industries, Newark, N.J.; Graphics: Duggal, New York City (3M photomurals); Furniture: NJS Carpentry Inc., Union City, N.J.; Props/decoratives: Golden Oldies, Flushing, N.Y.; Mannequins/forms: Pucci International, New York City

"DO AS YOU LIKE"
ZCMI, SALT LAKE CITY

Mike Stephens, visual director; Tim Davis, designer; Dennis Wardle and
Alysa Revell, project team

◆

Faux finishes of burled wood — on panels, pedestal and gift box —
set the tone for these Father's Day windows. Staggered panels
provide depth and a backdrop for men's forms, while shoes,
accessories and scent are featured with the props.

◆

Suppliers: Halo Lighting, Elk Grove Village, Ill.; Bernstein Display, Astoria,
N.Y.; Dixon Paper, Salt Lake City; Oasis Stage Works, Salt Lake City

TOMMY HILFIGER
ZCMI, SALT LAKE CITY

Mike Stephens, visual director; Tim Davis, designer

◆

In launching Tommy Hilfiger's new cologne, "Tommy" artwork was screened onto silk panels. Antique tables were incorporated into windows to tie Tommy's ready-to-wear into the launch. Interior presentation also featured the screened panels and fashion merchandise. Blue and white stars were affixed to the floor to lead customers to the Tommy counter.

◆

Suit form: Bernstein Display, Astoria, N.Y. Lighting: Halo Lighting, Elk Grove Village, Ill. (Halo Lighting) Furniture: Anthony's Antiques, Salt Lake City Signage: ZCMI, Salt Lake City Graphics: Tommy Hilfiger, Lagoona Nigule, Calif.

DENNIS POTTS, SALT LAKE CITY

BIGSBY & KRUTHERS
OAKBROOK CENTER
OAKBROOK, ILL.

Bigsby & Kruthers, Chicago: Darrel Loyd, former vice president of developement and visual merchandising; Karen Foley, former design assistant

◆

This Bigsby & Kruthers men's store uses a materials palette of rich mahogany woods, oak, maple, limestone, leather, suede, steel and marble to create a suitably masculine environment. Curves and soft undulations, including a dramatic S-curved mahogany shoe-wall, contribute to a contemporary atmosphere. Wire forms along the escalator offer a lighthearted change of pace from traditional mannequins.

◆

Architect: Cowan & Associates, Columbus, Ohio; General contractor: Richter + Ratner Contracting, Maspeth, N.Y.; Lighting design: Superior Lighting, Chicago; Fixturing: Seven Continents, Toronto; E-J Industries, Chicago; Design Industries, Indianapolis; Furniture: Luminaire, Chicago; Room & Board, Chicago; Design Link Int'l.; Niedermaier, Chicago; Flooring: Durkan, Dalton, Ga.; Pande, Camerom & Co., New York City; Dialogica, New York City; Ann Sacks Tile & Stone, Portland, Ore.; Wall coverings: Innovations, New York City; Signage: Signtech, Lemon Grove, Calif.; ALU, New York City (sign holders); Props/decoratives: J&R Collection, New York City; Mannequins/forms: Pucci Int'l., New York City; George Dell Inc., New York City; Greneker, Los Angeles; Custom art: Sid Dickens & Associates, Vancouver, B.C.; Custom stair rails: Eberting Associates, Three Oaks, Mich.; Faux finishing: James Mobley, Chicago

EDDIE BAUER
SAN FRANCISCO

FRCH Design Worldwide, Cincinnati: James Fitzgerald, chair and ceo; Kevin Roche, partner-in-charge; Barb Fabing, design principal; Tom Horwitz, project principal; Tony Nasser, project architect; Terri Altenau and Jason Watts, designers. Eddie Bauer team: John Wyatt, vice president of real estate; Mike Miller, director of store design; Bill McDermid, director of store planning and construction; Kevin Gysler, manager of store planning and construction; Norm Johnson, project manager, design; Joe Scheiner, project manager, construction; Jane McCartin, manager of purchasing; Frank Kennard, divisional vice president of visual presentation; Joe Stoneburnger, director of visual presentation; Bill Johnston, manager of visual operations

◆

Located in the landmark Gump's building, the store's three-level, 28,600-square-foot interior was gutted and restructured. Communicating the store's lifestyle identity are large-scale backlit graphics of West Coast nature, as well as iron-detailed chandeliers. Each level employs rich natural materials, including wood, metal and leather. Stone from the Northwest is used for aisleway flooring.

◆

Lighting consultant: Ross De Alessi Lighting Design, Seattle; General contractor: Jim McClymonds, RAS Builders, San Francisco; Fixturing: Synsor Corp., Woodinville, Wash.; Design Industries, Indianapolis; Omaha Fixtures, Omaha, Neb.; Eurotek, Kent, Wash.; Flooring: Western Tile, Bellevue, Wash. (tile); R.J. Pitcher, Liverpool, N.Y. (wood); Zickgraf (wood); PermaGrain, Media Pa. (wood); Applied Radiant Energy Corp., Forest, Va. (wood); Gammapar, Forest, Va. (wood); Carpet Technical Services, Collegeville, Pa. (carpet); Ceiling tile and grid: Sepia Interior Supply, Seattle; Lighting: Charles Loomis Inc., Kirkland, Wash.; Villa Lighting, St. Louis; Brass Light Gallery, Milwaukee; Wall coverings: MDC Wallcoverings, Vernon, Calif. (wall paper); Signage and graphics: Turner Exhibits, Edmond, Wash. (custom signage and storefront); Color 2000, San Francisco (lighted graphics); Image National, Boise, Idaho (storefront); Precis Architectural, Kirkland, Wash. (interior); Messenger Signs, Seattle; Props: Can Am Trading, Greenfield, Mass.; Golden Oldies, Flushing, N.Y.; Custom millwork: LaBruna Industries, Ontario; Store Kraft, Beatrice, Neb.; Materials: Matheus Lumber, Woodinville, Wash. (truss and trellis lumber)

PAUL BIELENBERG, LOS ANGELES

ANN TAYLOR
MADISON AVENUE
NEW YORK CITY

Desgrippes Gobe & Associates, New York City: Marc Gobe, principal; Wendy Hald, creative director; Ray Shick, Werner Franz and Mary Meuer, designers; Cheryl Kenny, design director (former)

◆

In the retailer's new flagship, merchandise is presented on fixtures with sensual shapes rendered in bronze, stone, frosted green glass and auburn wood. Sculptural details on fixtures, door handles and railings fit together with natural materials and display panels.

◆

General contractor: Fisher Development Inc.; Fixtures: Arbor Store Interiors, Toronto; Lighting design: Auerbach Glasow, San Francisco

ANDREW BORDWIN, NEW YORK CITY

ACCESSORIES

Smaller merchandise — jewelry, perfumes, sunglasses, shoes and bodycare products — requires a focused approach to visual merchandising. Drawing the eye to a pair of earrings poses different challenges than those involved in illustrating an apparel collection. ◆ Repetition is one technique you'll see represented in this chapter — positioning identical backlit crystal perfume bottles in framed vignettes or organizing rows of lotions (or shoes, or eyewear frames or purses) on feature shelves. Saks introduced a new perfume from Estee Lauder by emphasizing the shape of individual bottles behind 15 ovals cut-out from a metal panel. Another approach takes one small piece of merchandise — a single shoe, necklace or pair of earrings — and presents it as precious in a setting designed to focus all attention on this one element. O.C. Tanner, for example, presented individual necklaces and matching earrings on spotlighted bust forms. Carved pedestals lift the forms to a comfortable viewing height, while floral headdresses raise the presentation beyond the ordinary. ◆ You'll also see an emphasis on identifying signage in this section, ranging from simple window lettering to enlargements of packaging and designer logos. The Rockport Store and Kids Foot Locker in particular make generous use of lifestyle graphics. Lighting also plays in important role, as seen in Morgenthal-Frederics Optitions. Vendor-supplied materials are cleverly incorporated into perfume launches and shoe presentations. And in Easy Spirit's re-imaged store, urban architectural graphics and product information signage combine to form backdrops for shoe shelving.

O.C. Tanner, Salt Lake City

"SPRING IS IN THE HAIR"
O.C. TANNER
SALT LAKE CITY

Brent Erkelens, visual merchandising director; Virginia Wallin and Rosie Burbidge, store team

◆

Mounted on poles at eye level, O.C. Tanner dressed bust forms with fantastic headdresses of silk flowers, then placed them in fields of real potted flowers. Pin spots highlighted the jewelry from above.

◆

Forms: Greneker, Los Angeles

BORGE ANDERSEN, SALT LAKE CITY

144

ANN TAYLOR FLAGSHIP COSMETICS
MADISON AVENUE
NEW YORK CITY

Desgrippes Gobe & Associates, New York City: Marc Gobe, principal;
Wendy Hald, creative director; Ray Shick, Werner Franz and Mary Meuer,
designers; Cheryl Kenny, design director

◆

In the retailer's new flagship, merchandise is presented on fixtures
with sensual shapes rendered in bronze, stone, frosted green glass
and auburn wood. Sculptural details on fixtures, door handles and
railings fit together with natural materials and display panels.

◆

General contractor: Fisher Development Inc., San Francisco; Fixtures: Arbor
Store Interiors, Toronto; Lighting design: Auerbach Glasow, San Francisco

"ESTEE LAUDER PLEASURES"
SAKS FIFTH AVENUE
NEW YORK CITY

William Viets, vice president visual merchandising; Michael Salinas, visual merchandise director, Ward Garee, visual merchandise manager; Poppy Burns, manager special projects
New York Store Team: Terry Jacobs, director; Paula Coccimiglio, assistant director; Donna Harris, manager; Steven Slomowitz, stylist
New York Window Team: Randall Yaw, window manager; Gregg Ballwegg, lighting specialist, Martin Nederpelt, production manager; Steven Swersak, fashion stylist

◆

The launch of Estee Lauder's "Pleasure" was based on a color palette of pastel pink and satin silver metal. Windows were planned with ellipsoidal openings backlit with pastel pink lights. The openings held perfume bottles floating on acrylic risers. Outpost kiosks used a similar concept in metal with half-ellipsoidal acrylic shelves. Tabletops of frosted acrylic were screened with the logo in silver and featured pink American Beauty roses, large-scale images and a wash of multicolored pink lights.

◆

Signage: Esto Graphics, New York City; Props: Sama Plastics, Carlstadt, N.J. (table toppers)

"MURANO 'EAU DE MURANO'"
SAKS FIFTH AVENUE, NEW YORK CITY

William Viets, vice president visual merchandising; Michael Salinas, visual merchandise director, Ward Garee, visual merchandise manager; Poppy Burns, manager special projects
New York Store Team: Terry Jacobs, director; Paula Coccimiglio, assistant director; Donna Harris, manager; Steven Slomowitz, stylist
New York Window Team: Randall Yaw, window manager; Gregg Bullwegg, lighting specialist, Martin Nederpelt, production manager; Steven Swersak, fashion stylist
Consultant: Michelle Pontzaccia, Murano

◆

Venetian blown glass from the island of Murano was the focus of this launch in a marriage of fragrance and fine art. The Doge palace in Venice sets the backdrop in custom-painted imagery, lit to look antique; fragmented capitals each present a single large factice. Inside, a custom shop environment housed multiples of product ranging from objets d'art, vessels and bowls in Venetian glass to fragrance bottles and decanters.

◆

Signage: Esto Graphics, New York City; Vitrine and back walls: Murano

"DREAMBOAT"
O.C. TANNER
SALT LAKE CITY

Brent Erkelens, visual merchandising director; Virginia Wallin, store team

◆

This O.C. Tanner window display employs a toy boat and blue
acrylic for a pleasantly surreal visual pun.

◆

Water photograph: Cies Sexton, Denver

MORGENTHAL-FREDERICS OPTITIONS
MADISON AVENUE
NEW YORK CITY

Rockwell Architecture, Planning and Design, P.C. — David Rockwell,
principal, Kathleen Craig, project manager; Alice Yiu, director of interiors

◆

This Morgenthal-Frederics store is designed to complement and
reflect the design and functionality of the eyeglasses the store sells.
Shaker-style fixtures combine simplicity and elegance, while
oversized fixtures and mirrors bring a Through the Looking Glass
appeal to the store.

◆

Tables, cases and maple panels: Bronx Builders, Bronx, N.Y.; Custom lamps:
Sirmos, Long Island City; Window display cases, mirrors, chairs and stools:
John A. Savittieri Furniture, Wallington, N.J.

SPORTING EYES
TEMPE, ARIZ.

Habitat Inc., Tempe, Ariz. — Randy Chamberlain, president; Scott Hopman, vice president; Richard Schreiber, senior architectural designer; Ann McKenzie, senior interior architectural designer

◆

Sculpted figures of hot-white gesso — mountain biker, skier, fly fisherman and snowboarder — model the latest fashions in sunglasses. Also contributing to the action-packed atmosphere of the 800-square-foot store are intensely focused halogen lighting, vertical backlit signage and display cabinets faced in cantelope-stained maple veneer.

◆

Flooring: ICI, Roswell, Ga.; Lighting: Lighting Design Resource, Scottsdale, Ariz.; Signage: Royal Sign Co., Phoenix, Ariz.; Graphics, mannequins and forms: Habitat, Inc., Tempe, Ariz.

RICHARD SCHREIBER, TEMPE, ARIZ.

THE ROCKPORT STORE
COLUMBUS AVENUE
NEW YORK CITY

Desgrippes Gobe & Associates, New York City — Kenneth Hirst, creative director; Steve Schappacher, design director; Mark Oller, Amy Ingrassia, Werner Franz, senior designers; Mary Meuer, Victoria Kirk, project team; Anthony De Caria, environmental graphics; Phyllis Aragaki, creative director, lifestyle graphics team; Christopher Vice, design director, lifestyle graphics team

◆

Reflecting a campaign by parent company Reebok to revitalize Rockport's image as a source for comfortable men's shoes, the flagship employed variations of natural materials in a Maine-inspired color scheme of earthy neutrals, mossy greens and sky blues. Lifestyle graphics of casual, outdoors models draw attention to shoes presented against sandblasted plywood, stained particleboard, frosted glass and metals.

General contractor: GC Contractors, New York City; Lighting consultant: Lighting Management Inc., New York City; Fixtures: Bon-Art, Newark, N.J.; Greneker, Los Angeles; Flooring: Materials Marketing Co., Chicago (stone); Kiosk: Vira/Eastern Woodwork, Rahway, N.J.

ANDREW BORDWIN, NEW YORK CITY

EASY SPIRIT
MADISON AVENUE
NEW YORK CITY

Design Centre, Cincinnati

◆

In a move to a more sophisticated look, Easy Spirit placed its products against oversized duotoned photomurals identifying women's shoe collections for "city," "pathway," "beach" and "steps." Signage prominently features product benefits and information. The gentle curve of the new logo is repeated throughout the store in curved glass shelves and display stanchions.

Fixtures: Porter/Hillstead, Farmington, Conn.; Graphics: North American Signs, South Bend, Ind.

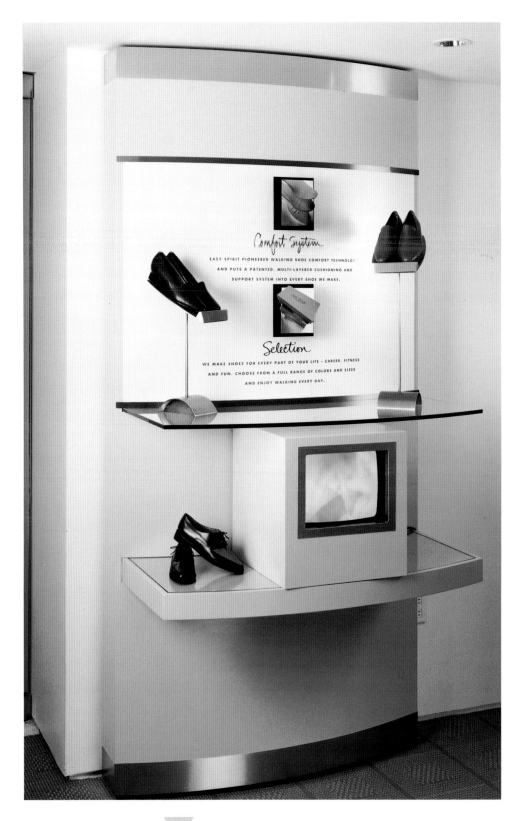

STRIDE RITE
CHESTNUT HILL MALL
CHESTNUT HILL, MASS.

◆

Elkus/Manfredi Architects, Ltd., Boston — Howard F. Elkus, partner; David P. Manfredi, partner and principal in charge; Elizabeth Lowrey Clapp, director of interior architecture; Laura Ulvestad, Tiffonie Milkowski, design team The Stride Rite Corp., Lexington, Mass. — Robert Siegel, chair and ceo; Jules Pieri, vice president strategic marketing; Tracy Zaslow, director store design and construction

Intended to appeal to children, this prototype features light wood casework and benches, a palette of primary colors dominated by blue and a series of kinetic and static sculptures. Point-of-purchase displays present and explain the different styles of shoes Stride Rite offers for growing kids. An overhead assembly-line track conveys several three-dimensional shoe puns, including a shoe-horn (with trumpet) and shoe tree (with branches)

◆

Graphics: Clifford Selbert Design, Cambridge, Mass.; Lighting: Illuminart, Ypsilanti, Mich.; Structural: McNamara/Salvia, Inc., Boston; Consulting engineer: Lottero + Mason Associates, Boston; Point-of-purchase displays: Thomas-Leeds, New York City; Ceiling: Armstrong, Lancaster, Pa.; Paint: Benjamin Moore, Montvale, N.J.; Fixturing/seating: Custom Surroundings, Inc., Cleveland; Flooring: Masland, Mobile, Ala. (carpet); Mannington Commercial, Calhoun, Ga. (vinyl composite tile); Johnsonite, Chagrin Falls, Ohio (vinyl base); Wall coverings: Martin Senour, Cleveland (accent paint); Fabrics: Innovations, New York City; Decoratives: PM Designs, Boston

"HOLIDAY IMAGE GRAPHICS"
KIDS FOOT LOCKER
SALT LAKE CITY

Bonneville Communications, Salt Lake City: Tracy Gregory, senior account executive; Edie Schoepp, production manager; Michelle Pilcher, project coordinator; Vincent Iannucci, director of marketing, Kids Foot Locker
Art Director: Stephanie Workman, Jungle Design, Salt Lake City

◆

In developing a program that can be updated three to four times a year by store personnel, Bonneville linked lifestyle phrases and photography. Shoewall graphics include print at the bottom that states the type of shoes displayed, reinforced by phrases for image and personality.

◆

Printer Broker: Pro Logic, Salt Lake City (printer); Film: Scanner Craft, Salt Lake City; Photographs: Erik Ostling and Mark Kidman, Salt Lake City

I have a dream.

FILA GRANT HILL

SCOTT TANNER, SALT LAKE CITY

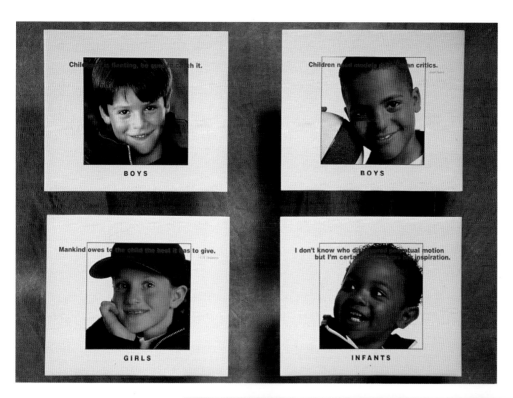

"TIFFANY NATURE"
TIFFANY & CO.
FIFTH AVENUE,
NEW YORK CITY

Robert Rufino, vice president visual merchandising, Tiffany & Co., New York City

◆

Windows presenting the Tiffany Nature line of exclusive fine jewelry, scarves and private-stock china, also tie into the company's nature sponsorships to charitable organizations in the New York region. Green grass, garden tools and statuary, wrought-iron gates and the first spring flowers provide a setting for Nature-inspired fine jewelry and accessories.

◆

Props: The Garden Room, New York City

"SILVER DEPARTMENT"
ZCMI, SALT LAKE CITY

Mike Stephens, visual director;
Dennis Wardle, designer

◆

Opulence is the order of the day
in this display for ZCMI's silver
department. Rich, coppery
curtains and local pebbles
provide the backdrop for
suspended silver.

◆

Fabrics: Dazian Fabrics, New York
City; Lighting: Halo Lighting, Elk
Grove Village, Ill.

DENNIS POTTS, SALT LAKE CITY

"ROBERT LEE MORRIS"
ZCMI, SALT LAKE CITY

Mike Stephens, visual director; Celeste Cecchini, designer

◆

Copper walls and careful lighting provide a shimmering backdrop
for Robert Lee Morris accessories. Purses, belts and jewelry are
presented on jersey-covered dressmaker forms.

◆

Flooring: Blast Spray Equipment Co., Salt Lake City; Lighting: Halo Lighting,
Elk Grove Village, Ill.; Wall coverings: Zims, Salt Lake City (copper tooling);
Mannequins/forms: Stockman Forms, New York City

ROBERT LEE MORRIS
DESIGNER ON TWO

DENNIS POTTS, SALT LAKE CITY

169

INDEX OF DESIGN FIRMS

INDEX OF STORES

Visual Merchandising and Store Design Books
available from ST Publications

Budget Guide to Retail Store Planning & Design
Jewelry on Display
Stores and Retail Spaces
Visual Merchandising and Store Design Workbook

For a complete catalog of related books and magazines, please contact:

ST Publications, Inc.
Book Division
407 Gilbert Avenue
Cincinnati, Ohio 45202

Tel. 513-421-2050
Fax 513-421-6110